FULL DISCLOSURE

Everything the Bible Says About Financial Giving

by Herb Miller

DISCIPLESHIP RESOURCES
PO BOX 340003 • NASHVILLE, TN 37203-0003
www.discipleshipresources.org

Cover and book design by Joey McNair

Edited by Linda R. Whited and Cindy S. Harris

ISBN 0-88177-411-1

Library of Congress Control Number 2003106195

DR411

Contents

Introduction 5

Part I: Why Should We Give? 9

Theme 1: Financial Giving Puts God First 11

Theme 2: Financial Giving Worships God 17

Theme 3: Financial Giving Expresses Thankfulness to God 23

Theme 4: Financial Giving Acts as God's Steward 27

Theme 5: Financial Giving Supports God's Long-Range Goals 31

Theme 6: Financial Giving Motivates Others to Put God First 39

Theme 7: Financial Giving to God Must Include Helping People in Need 43

Theme 8: Financial Giving to God Must Include Right Living 47

Part II: How Does Giving Benefit Us? 51

Theme 9: Financial Giving Reflects Trust in God's Providence 53

Theme 10: Financial Giving Protects Against Materialistic Idolatry 57

Theme 11: Financial Giving Brings Rewards 61

Part III: How Should We Give? 65

Theme 12: Give Intentionally 67

Theme 13: Give Proportionately 71

Theme 14: Give Regularly 73

Theme 15: Give One Tenth 75

Theme 16: Give Generously 81

Theme 17: Give Sacrificially 85

Theme 18: Give Without Pride 89

Theme 19: Give Without Selfish Motives 91

Theme 20: Give Joyfully 93

Appendix I 97

Appendix II 109

Appendix III 111

Appendix IV 114

Appendix V 116

Appendix VI 119

Appendix VII 121

Appendix VIII 122

Appendix IX 124

Appendix X 126

INTRODUCTION

The Bible reports spiritual experiences, insights, and wisdom from the major characters in a two-thousand-year drama recorded in sixty-six writings (books) of the Old Testament and New Testament. Scholars have long noted that many spiritual truths that the Bible's heroes and heroines saw dimly in the opening pages of Genesis evolved into sharper focus over the centuries.

Throughout the Bible, its sages viewed financial giving as an important element in building and maintaining a spiritual relationship with God. Convictions regarding that connection started with Israelite thinking in approximately 1900 B.C., appeared in written form with the Genesis 40 Cain and Abel story, and concluded with Christian writings in approximately A.D. 90. Like the facets of a diamond, twenty financial stewardship themes appear, recur, and evolve across two thousand years. *Full Disclosure*

- identifies those twenty financial giving themes;
- lists all of the biblical texts that illustrate each of the twenty themes;
- gives the approximate writing date for each text;
- thumbnails the approximate historical setting of each text;
- notes how some of the twenty themes evolved and matured over time;
- provides reflection questions for group discussion.

Full Disclosure serves clergy, congregations, and all Christians in several ways. First, this book helps fill the information vacuum on the topic of what the Bible says about financial giving. National research shows that sixty-five percent of church members say the Bible contains valuable teachings about money, yet only nineteen percent say they have thought much about those teachings during the past twelve months. (See *The Crisis in the Churches: Spiritual Malaise, Fiscal Woe*, by Robert Wuthnow; Oxford University Press, 1997; page 140.) At least part of the reason for this lack of teaching stems from the absence of a comprehensive, definitive resource on what the Bible says about money.

Second, *Full Disclosure* helps Christians move beyond the misconception that financial stewardship's primary purpose is to raise funds that balance church budgets. Giving to God is always about ministry, not money. Giving to God is a spiritual endeavor, not a financial effort. Every encouragement toward financial giving stands on the foundation of Jesus' Great Commandment and Great Commission (Matthew 28:19-20; Luke 10:25-37; Acts 2:41-42), which may be summarized as follows:

- Grow spiritually in your relationship with God.
- Love your neighbors in church, community, and world.
- Offer Christ to people outside your church's walls.

Attempting to involve a high percentage of church members and attendees in generous financial giving habits is more than fundraising. It is not just a way to gain financial support for the congregation's budget. Financial giving fosters people's spiritual health by encouraging them in discipleship behaviors.

Third, *Full Disclosure* provides tools to help leaders facilitate spiritual growth through generous giving habits. Research indicates that churches in which pastors preach one message a year about money experience larger per capita giving than churches in which no financial stewardship preaching occurs. Churches in which pastors preach two or more consecutive messages about financial giving receive greater per capita donations than churches in which pastors preach one giving message per year. These congregations are also twice as likely to experience increased giving compared with the previous year's total. Congregations in which pastors preach a series of messages about giving are almost two-and-one-half times more likely to increase their giving than congregations in which pastors speak about giving in one sermon at a time, scattered across the year. (See *How to Increase Giving in Your Church*, by George Barna; Regal Books, 1997; pages 92–93.)

Yet, despite the spiritual-growth value of financial giving and its power to fund missions and ministries that accomplish Jesus' Great Commandment and Great Commission, many clergy fear—and therefore avoid talking about—money in the church. Some pastors seem to feel that this subject is

(a) beneath their theological dignity, (b) something the lay leaders ought to take care of, (c) dangerous to their tenure security with that congregation, or (d) all of the above.

Other pastors take pride in preaching and teaching biblical truth on every subject except money because (a) they fear sounding legalistic about tithing, (b) they fear coming across as judgmental of people with poor giving habits, (c) they fear that people might think they are covertly trying to engineer a salary increase, (d) they fear pushing church members to giving levels beyond their financial means, (e) they prefer not to consider improving their own personal giving habits, or (f) all of the above.

Pastors who do not buy into those myths and self-defense rationalizations, and/or pastors who are "in recovery" from them, need a biblical resource for this section of their preaching and teaching ministry. Clergy, lay leaders, and teachers often ask where to find group study and discussion material on financial giving to God. Yet pastors across the country report sparse crops of such resources.

Stewardship sermons and Bible studies bear more fruit if they speak in the many voices in which Scripture speaks. *Full Disclosure* lets us hear all twenty of the financial stewardship teachings in the Bible, not just the three or four that come to most people's minds.

Each of these twenty financial giving themes has roots in Israelite or Christian thinking from particular calendar years. However, like contemporary historians, few biblical writers put pen to scroll during the same year that history happened. Like writers of American or European history, not until years, decades, and sometimes even centuries later did leaders recognize the importance of events and write about those events and ideas stemming from them.

Scholars agree on the date some biblical books were written and the authorship of those books because they mention facts and experiences confirmed by the record of secular history, such as the years during which world rulers reigned. Scholarly guesses regarding the dates of other biblical writings vary widely. With a few exceptions, such as the dating of Isaiah, scholars less often dispute the sequence in which the biblical books were authored. Fortunately, for the purpose of this financial giving research, the sequence of biblical writings is more important than the exact year or decade each book was written.

Full Disclosure's dates and writing sequence rely on a wide range of books and scholarly opinions, including the *Good News Bible: The Bible in Today's English Version*, Second Edition (Thomas Nelson, Publishers, 1992) and *The One-Year Chronological Bible* (Tyndale House Publishers, 1995).

The Old Testament quotations come from the *Good News Bible*, and the New Testament quotations come from the New Revised Standard Version. For financial giving Scriptures whose meaning seems fuzzy, my primary scholarly source is *The New Interpreter's Bible*, Volumes 1–12 (Abingdon Press, 1994–2002). The twenty themes, their evolving maturation, and their spiritual application for contemporary Christians derive from the author's research and personal opinion.

Since the Bible's twenty financial giving themes answer three questions, *Full Disclosure* fits its Scripture citations into three sections:

1. Why Should We Give?
2. How Does Giving Benefit Us?
3. How Should We Give?

At times, these three headings seem arbitrary: Some Scripture quotations address two or all three questions. Therefore, a few verses show up as examples in more than one of the twenty themes.

Like Sergeant Friday in the 1950's television drama, *Full Disclosure*'s objective is to state "just the facts, ma'am, just the facts." *Full Disclosure* attempts to faithfully report every Old Testament and New Testament mention of financial giving to God. Achieving that goal is complex. The Bible is saturated with this topic. Amazingly large percentages of the Old Testament and New Testament discuss the relationship between financial giving and spiritual relationship with God. Thus, some readers may see financial giving implied in an uncited text. Thoroughness was attempted. Readers can decide whether achievement matched aspiration.

For group discussion or sermon preparation purposes, read *Full Disclosure* with a Bible handy. Accompanying most financial giving texts is a brief description of the text's setting and meaning. Every financial giving text is cited, but space does not permit quoting the entire story or historical context when each giving statement appears. Quoting in totality the settings in which the cited verses appear would move *Full Disclosure* from study-guide size into the unabridged dictionary category.

For maximum understanding and absorption of *Full Disclosure*'s insights, read and discuss each of the twenty financial giving themes with a group, using the following reflection questions:

1. In what ways do today's Christians affirm and live out this financial giving theme?
2. In what ways do today's Christians sometimes disregard this theme?
3. In what ways do today's church leaders sometimes disregard this theme?
4. How does this financial giving theme apply to you personally?

Part I

Why Should We Give?

Theme 1

Financial Giving Puts God First

harried church secretary accidentally typed this mistake in the worship bulletin's opening hymn title: "Holy, Holy, Holy, Lord Gold Almighty."

Her typographical error creates an excellent six-word sermon. Throughout its pages, the Bible keeps repeating this theme: Putting the God of Abraham, Isaac, Moses, and Jesus first in your life's priorities brings you many valuable benefits. You are tempted to put competing idols and/or ideological gods first in your life's priorities, which brings many negative consequences.

Your financial giving is not the only measure of whether you put God first in your priorities. Putting God first also involves right thinking, right behavior, right relationships with people, and right relationships with God. In other words, putting God first includes but is not limited to putting God first with your money. Financial giving is more than money, but it is not less than money. From beginning to end, the Bible says that your financial giving pattern illustrates your willingness or unwillingness to give yourself wholeheartedly to God's guidance in all of your life. Your money represents you. You exchange time, intelligence, abilities, and energy for the money you receive. How you use that money states what you believe is important in life. Thus, financial giving is an essential element in helping you form, retain, and grow in your spiritual connection with God.

The first instances of financial giving in the early Old Testament refer to human interaction with God approximately thirty-nine hundred years ago. During that era, people did not hold their financial assets in currency, bank accounts, stocks, and bonds. During the years when the Bible first reports people giving financially to God, wealth was primarily computed in livestock, grain, and wine. Contemporary Americans measure wealth in money. Ancient Israelites measured wealth in cattle (which can become food), grain (which can become bread), and wine (which can accompany meals). Thus, the burnt offerings and sacrifices that people gave to God as reported in the Old Testament are equal to putting your check in the offering plate to support the benevolences, missions, and ministries that God accomplishes through your congregation.

Genesis, the name of the Old Testament's first book, means origin. Genesis reports many origins, including (a) the creation of the universe and human beings, (b) the beginning of sin and suffering, (c) God's way of dealing with people as shown in the Israelites' early ancestors, and (d) the first record of giving money to God. Most scholars believe that scribes during Moses' era (many believe around 1290–1250 B.C.) formed the Bible's first five books—Genesis, Exodus, Leviticus, Numbers, and Deuteronomy—by reconstructing a variety of written sources as well as transferring to written form memorized accounts that had been transmitted around campfires and in other settings for generations and centuries beforehand.

Genesis 4:3-5 (about 1290–1250 B.C.) records the Bible's first mention of offerings to God. These verses leave unsolved the mystery of why God accepts Abel's offering and rejects Cain's offering. Readers must supply the answer with their imaginations. Most scholars assume that Cain's offering was somehow selfish, failing to genuinely honor God, since that warning reappears throughout the other five books from that era and all the other biblical sources. God asks for more than an offering; he asks for the heart of the person who gives the offering.

Genesis 8:20-21 (about 1290–1250 B.C.) tells of Noah building an altar and using animals and birds as a burnt offering to God at the end of the flood that covers the earth. "The odor of the sacrifice pleased the LORD." In this passage, as in many others throughout the Old Testament, Moses and the Israelites give God anthropomorphic qualities; they assume God smells things the same way humans do. The underlying point of this story and all subsequent offerings is that Noah put God first in his life.

Genesis 14:17-20 (about 1290–1250 B.C.) shows Abram putting God first with money, ahead of what Abram owed the king of Sodom and the allies who helped conquer Chedorlaomer and other pagan kings in the region God had promised to give Abram and his descendants. Abram gives Melchizedek, who is both a king and "a priest of the Most High God," "a tenth of all the loot he had recovered" in the conquest.

Exodus 22:29-30 (about 1290–1250 B.C.) illustrates some of the earliest religious rules God gives through Moses, rules that the Israelites call "The Law" or "The Law of Moses." God requires them to put God first by giving offerings from grain, wine, and olive oil in their season and by giving first-born sons and the first-born of their oxen and sheep.

The Law's multiple sections unfold across pages of the first five Old Testament books (the Pentateuch). The Law provides Israel with spiritual, communal, and legal regulations regarding daily living, worshiping God, and maintaining a right relationship with God. These numerous Law Scriptures provide rules, prescriptions, and practices the Israelites are to follow in putting God first in their lives. The Law includes (a) policies and general statements and (b) the procedures by which to apply these policies in specific situations. Embedded in these numerous Scriptures that comprise "the Law" are many instructions that tell the Israelites to put God first in their financial giving.

In addition to and different from the tithe (giving ten percent of your income to God), the law prescribes numerous other kinds of offerings and sacrifices designed to bring people into, and keep them in, a right relationship with God. These offerings and sacrifices give God thanks and praise, usually for a specific religious ceremony, festival, or other special purpose. Some of the offerings and sacrifices accompany confession of sin and guilt. All of them take the form of an offering or sacrifice of monetary worth made to God.

These two words—*offering* and *sacrifice*—are almost always used interchangeably in the Old Testament. *Sacrifice*, however, sometimes denotes a special offering that is burnt or slaughtered as a blood sacrifice and/or a sacrifice by fire. Scattered throughout the Old Testament and illustrated more than one hundred times, the various offerings and sacrifices include burnt offerings, whole burnt offerings, cereal offerings, meal offerings, meat offerings, drink offerings, fire offerings, heave offerings, wave offerings, offering of the first fruits, offering of honey, water offerings, sin offerings, peace offerings, thank offerings, votive offerings, trespass offerings, guilt offerings, and memorial offerings.

See Appendix I for a list of every instance in which the Law spells out six subthemes of "Financial Giving Puts God First."

A. Annual, Monthly, Weekly, Daily, and Special Offerings Put God First.
B. Giving the Sabbath Puts God First.

C. Idol Worship Puts God Last. (Many Old Testament and New Testament books state and illustrate this recurring theme: (1) God calls the people to worship God alone, not to worship God plus other gods. (2) Israel and its people promise to worship God alone. (3) Israel and its people fail to keep their promise. (4) Israel and its people reap disastrous consequences for adding idol worship to their God worship. (5) Israel and its people stop worshiping idols and focus on God alone. (6) The cycle repeats itself and repeats itself and . . .)
D. Human Sacrifice Puts God Last.
E. Putting God Last Reaps Negative Consequences.
F. Repenting of Putting God Last Brings Forgiveness.

Exodus 34:19-20, 26 (about 1290–1250 B.C.) records God renewing the covenant with the Israelites. God reminds them of the annual festivals and the requirement that they give God their firstborn sons, firstborn male livestock, and first grains that they harvest. "No one is to appear before me without an offering."

Deuteronomy 15:19-20 (about 1290–1250 B.C.) during Moses' era reiterates the rule that Israelites "set aside for the LORD your God all the first-born males of your cattle and sheep." However, the Israelites are now instructed to "eat them in the LORD's presence at the one place of worship." (Is this the origin of congregational potluck dinners—community meals eaten in the context of a spiritual focus?)

Mark 12:41-44 (about A.D. 55–65). Jesus is seated at a place where people put offerings into the Temple treasury. He says that the large amounts the rich people gave were not worth as much in their totality as the penny a poor widow gave, because "she out of her poverty has put in everything she had, all she had to live on." Here again, the Bible asserts that giving is a matter of the heart. God measures generosity by people's willingness to give an appropriate percentage of their financial means, not by the amount they give. (This story is repeated in Luke 21:1-4.)

Luke 11:42 (about A.D. 60). Jesus says that God condemns people for giving ten percent of their income without living righteously. Jesus says they should do both: live righteously and give ten percent.

Matthew 5:17-20 (about A.D. 60–65). Jesus emphasizes that the letter of the Old Testament Law is important, but the spirit of the heart and right actions must accompany conformance to that letter of the Law. Jesus sees that many Pharisees and teachers of the Old Testament Law know its words but do not live them. Jesus says this prevents these leaders from entering the kingdom of heaven (*kingdom of God* and *kingdom of heaven* are synonymous terms throughout the New Testament). This teaching correlates with

Luke 11:42, where Jesus affirms the tithe of one's income but says that people must also have righteous actions toward one another, not just give ten percent of their incomes.

Matthew 23:23-24 (about A.D. 60–65). Jesus restates an emphasis from earlier in his teaching ministry. He says that people should do "justice and mercy and faith" *and* give ten percent of their spice crop (mint, dill, and cumin). Financial giving and right living toward God and other people must go together.

Acts 7:39-43 (about A.D. 63–70) is part of the history of the early church's expansion and describes Stephen's sermon to the Sanhedrin. He reminds them that their ancestors offered sacrifices to a calf they made instead of bringing God "sacrifices forty years in the wilderness," and God banished them to Babylon as punishment. Giving offerings *to God* is important, not just giving offerings to anything. Giving to gods of people's own choosing does not equal putting God first by giving to God.

A college student was struggling with tough choices regarding his future. In a conference with his professor he asked, "What do you think I should do with my life?" The professor replied, "You are smart and capable. You can be successful at just about anything you decide you want to do. Just be sure not to miss the main thing!" "What do you mean?" the student asked. "What is the main thing?" The professor replied, "Your own life."

Jesus repeatedly warned his students (disciples) of the same danger: missing the main thing. Jesus says life centered on God brings meaning, purpose, and satisfaction; life centered on something other than God creates the opposite result. Jesus says money is more than money: Misusing money seduces you into choosing a destructive life focus. Proper use of money moves you toward a productive, meaningful life focus.

How has your financial giving helped you find the main thing in life?

Questions for Reflection

1. In what ways do today's Christians affirm and live out the theme that financial giving puts God first?
2. In what ways do today's Christians sometimes disregard this theme?
3. In what ways do today's church leaders sometimes disregard this theme?
4. How does this financial giving theme apply to you personally?

Theme 2
Financial Giving Worships God

Church leaders, members, and people who teach financial stewardship tend to view the relationship between financial giving and worship in two different ways. Some churches try to avoid any mention of money during worship. A few churches no longer pass offering plates during the worship service. They put a box in the foyer or at the back of the sanctuary. People put their money in the box before or after worship. Leaders in such churches seem to think worship is more "spiritual" if they refrain from mixing money with it.

Other pastors say, "I think that is a travesty—a gross misunderstanding of what the offering is. We pass the offering plate as a significant part of worship here. The offering is as important a part of worship as prayer, as music, as Scripture, and as preaching" (Sermon by Rev. Bill Couch, January 2002; LakeRidge United Methodist Church, Lubbock, Texas). Couch's statement stands on a firm biblical foundation. Scripture provides no rationale for excluding offerings from worship or for feeling apologetic about receiving offerings during worship services. Just the opposite! In twenty-five places throughout the spiritual history in its pages, the Bible equates financial giving to God with worshiping God.

Genesis 8:20-22 (about 1290–1250 B.C.) records the earliest Israelite history during Moses' era. This history was probably extracted from memorized oral sources. Several Genesis passages associate financial giving with worship of the Israelite God. This passage tells of Noah building an altar at the end of the flood and worshiping God by giving animals and birds as burnt offerings.

Genesis 14:17-20 (about 1290–1250 B.C.) describes what happened following Abram's victory over Chedorlaomer and other pagan kings in conquest of the lands God had promised Abram and his descendants. Melchizedek, "a priest of the Most High God," conducts what appears to be a religious ceremony involving bread and wine. After blessing Abram, Melchizedek says, "May the Most High God, who gave you victory over your enemies, be praised!"

Genesis 35:1-3, 9-15 (about 1290–1250 B.C.). At an ancient sacred place with many oak trees, Jacob worships and receives God's promise of many blessings. Jacob seems to promise to keep his family separated from worship of pagan gods. God promises blessings on Jacob and his descendants. At this location where God spoke to him, "Jacob set up a memorial stone and consecrated it by pouring wine and olive oil on it. He named the place Bethel." (This stone is different from the memorial stone Jacob erected to his wife Rachel in 35:20, when she died on the road to Ephrath, now called Bethlehem.)

Exodus 18:1-12 (about 1290–1250 B.C.). Following the Israelites' escape from Egyptian slavery, Moses visits his father-in-law, Jethro, the priest of Midian. Moses reports to Jethro "everything that the Lord had done to the king and the people of Egypt in order to rescue the Israelites." "Then Jethro brought an offering to be burned whole and other sacrifices to be offered to God; and Aaron and all the leaders of Israel went with him to eat the sacred meal as an act of worship." Thus a financial gift and a sacred meal are combined in worship, as happens innumerable times throughout the Old Testament and is repeated with a new twist throughout the New Testament—as for example in the Lord's Supper. Christ symbolically replaces the animal sacrifices the Hebrews brought as sin offerings to their worship's sacred meal. As John the Baptist put it, "Here is the Lamb of God who takes away the sin of the world! . . . This is the Son of God" (John 1:29, 34). As the apostle Paul put it, "For our paschal lamb, Christ, has been sacrificed" (1 Corinthians 5:7b).

Exodus 20:22-24 (about 1290–1250 B.C.). The Lord instructs Moses to tell the Israelites, "Make an altar of earth for me, and on it sacrifice your sheep and your cattle as offerings to be completely burned and as fellowship offerings. In every place that I set aside for you to worship me, I will come to you and bless you."

Exodus 23:14-15 (about 1290–1250 B.C.). The Lord says that during the three great Israelite festivals of each year, the people should "never come to worship me without bringing an offering." These three festivals are the Festival of Unleavened Bread, the Harvest Festival, and the Festival of Shelters.

Leviticus 9:8-22 (about 1290–1250 B.C.) shows that in addition to the peoples' offerings, the priests gave personal offerings at the first worship service outside God's just-completed tent. This is *the earliest but not the only biblical indication* that God does not exempt clergy from financial giving. (See Numbers 18:25-30.)

Deuteronomy 12:11-27 (about 1290–1250 B.C.) warns the Israelites not to offer their sacrifices to God or their tithes and offerings in a place of their own choosing. They "must offer them only in the one place that the LORD will choose in the territory of one of your tribes." This is *the earliest illustration* that the Bible does not say that people can worship God anyplace—in the woods, hunting, fishing, at the beach, in the mountains, and so forth.

1 Samuel 1:3-10 (about 586–539 B.C.), written during the Israelites' Exile in Babylon, describes the period between the judges and the monarchy under King David. This passage describes a time during which the Israelite, Elkanah, went annually to worship and offer sacrifices at Shiloh. During this period, families customarily ate together in the house of the Lord as part of the worship. Is this the model from which churches developed potluck dinners?

1 Kings 3:2-4 (about 586–539 B.C.). First Kings, written during the Israelites' Exile in Babylon, continues 2 Samuel's coverage of King David's monarchy, which began around 1010 B.C., and that of his son Solomon, which ended around 931 B.C. This passage notes that the Israelites are offering sacrifices at many altars before King Solomon builds the Temple at Jerusalem.

Psalm 96:8 (about 539–500 B.C.). "Praise the LORD's glorious name; bring an offering and come into his Temple."

2 Chronicles 33:16-17 (about 430 B.C.). Second Chronicles picks up where 1 Chronicles leaves off and describes events from approximately 970–586 B.C., the beginning of King Solomon's rule to the Babylonian Exile after the fall of Jerusalem. This passage reports King Manasseh repenting and restoring the giving of fellowship offerings and thanksgiving offerings at the Temple. A dramatic footnote to that incident: Although the people continued to offer sacrifices at other places of worship, they offered them only to the Lord. At this point in history, the religious leaders thought people could worship God and give offerings in more than one location simultaneously. This opinion was a dramatic change from the days when they believed that God was anthropomorphic (like a person, only available in one location at a time). Earlier, in Joshua 22:10-34, the Israelites were prepared to go to war with other Israelites who attempted to worship God at multiple sites.

See Appendix II for additional biblical references on the theme "Financial Giving Worships God." See Appendix III for its two subthemes:

A. Proper Offering Preparation Helps People Worship.
B. Proper Offering Equipment Helps People Worship.

Mark 11:15-17 (about A.D. 55–65). Jesus drives out of the Temple the merchants who are buying and selling there, the moneychangers, and people selling doves to the worshipers. Jesus forbids anyone to carry merchandise through the Temple courts. He quotes from Isaiah 56:7, saying God's house should be called "a house of prayer for all the nations," but the chief priests and teachers of the Law have made it "a den of robbers." Jesus is once again saying, as he often does, that authentic giving is a matter of heart attitude (prayer centered) and a matter of worship (God focused), not merely a matter of fulfilling a ritual by purchasing doves to be sacrificed. (This story is repeated in Luke 19:45-46 [written about A.D. 60] and in Matthew 21:12-13 [written about A.D. 60–65].)

Jesus said he came that we might have life (John 10:10). He did not say that he came so that we can have religion. He did not even say that he came so that we can give offerings to support churches. Jesus came with the good news that God seeks each of us, asks us to wholeheartedly put God first in our lives, and promises positive benefits from such a life focus. That is the prime purpose of giving our money to God in worship—not merely so that the church can pay its bills or accomplish ministries but so that we do not put something else first, ahead of the God who can give us life that is abundant and whole.

Do your church leaders view the offering as a necessary evil? Have they reduced this awesome opportunity to a routine "passing the plate" to pay the church's bills? Do you sometimes hear remarks such as, "We wish we didn't have to do this; but after all, it takes money to run the church"?

Such quips have no place in congregations that gather to worship the God of Abraham, Isaac, and Jesus. Scripture views the offering as an essential element in authentic worship. When God's people lay their financial gifts on God's altar, they declare the "worth-ship" of God in their lives in a manner unequaled by other parts of the service. Even if your church's operating budget were fully endowed, you would still need to take an offering at every worship service. Without an offering, you park the train on a side track, robbing people of an opportunity to spiritually connect with God.

Questions for Reflection

1. In what ways do today's Christians affirm and live out the theme that financial giving worships God?
2. In what ways do today's Christians sometimes disregard this theme?
3. In what ways do today's church leaders sometimes disregard this theme?
4. How does this financial giving theme apply to you personally?

Theme 3

Financial Giving Expresses Thankfulness to God

Contemporary Christians replay the biblical tape of thankfulness in two principal ways: by financial giving that expresses thankfulness for spiritual blessings, and by financial giving that expresses thankfulness for material affluence.

Spiritual Thankfulness

James Denny, a great Scottish theologian of the last century, once said that he would like to go into every church in Scotland, hold up a cross, and shout to the people, "God loves like that!"

"Love so amazing, so divine, demands my soul, my life, my all," we sing in a great worship hymn. Does that "all" include a thankful response from our billfold or purse? If not, are we connecting with the God of Abraham, Isaac, and Jesus? Or are we connecting with the social custom of church attendance and membership?

The Bible's second book, Exodus, written approximately 1290–1250 B.C. during Moses' era, describes the escape of Israelite slaves who built some of Egypt's great pyramids. In the landscape of historical events to which every subsequent generation of Israelites looked back in thankfulness to God, this slave-freeing, nation-creating period stands like a giant redwood.

Paul reiterates this spiritual thanksgiving theme in 2 Corinthians 9:12, noted below.

Exodus 12:1-28 (about 1290–1250 B.C.) describes Moses and Aaron passing on God's instructions to all the people. They are to prepare bread without yeast to eat on this sacred day and all future celebrations of it, and "Each of you is to choose a lamb or a young goat and kill it, so that your families can celebrate Passover." After hearing the explanation that by wiping the blood of this gift to God on the doorposts and the beams above the doors of their houses, the Angel of Death would pass by the Israelites on the way to kill the Egyptian firstborns, "The Israelites knelt down and worshiped. Then they went and did what the LORD had commanded Moses and Aaron." This annual thanksgiving celebration by every succeeding generation honors God for this mighty act, by which the Egyptians were finally convinced to free the slaves and send them toward nationhood in the Promised Land of their forefather, Abraham.

Exodus 13:1-2, 11-16 (about 1290–1250 B.C.) instructs the Israelites to dedicate all first-born males, both of their animals and their children, to God in thankful remembrance of God delivering them from slavery in Egypt. However, for all their first-born male donkeys, they may substitute the offering of a lamb. They "must buy back every first-born male child." This may symbolically contrast with the time when, legally speaking, the Egyptian Pharaoh owned every first-born male. Now these boy babies belong to God.

Deuteronomy 26:1-11 (about 1290–1250 B.C.) during Moses' era instructs the Israelites to take the first part of each crop to the priest at the one place of worship and thankfully celebrate God's deliverance from Egyptian slavery.

Deuteronomy 27:1-7 (about 1290–1250 B.C.) instructs the Israelites to set up large stones, build an altar, and gratefully offer sacrifices the day they cross the Jordan River into the land God promised them.

Psalm 50:5-23 (about 970–931 B.C.) during King Solomon's era says God appreciates "your sacrifices and the burnt offerings you always bring me." Yet God wants the Israelites to offer more than those material assets. "Let the giving of thanks be your sacrifice to God, and give the Almighty all that you promised." After reprimanding the Israelites for unrighteous behavior, the chapter's last verse summarizes its main point: "Giving thanks is the sacrifice that honors me, and I will surely save all who obey me."

Psalm 116:13-19 (about 586–539 B.C.) during the Israelites' Babylonian Exile says, "I will bring a wine offering to the LORD, to thank him for saving me." The psalm concludes with, "I will give you a sacrifice of thanksgiving and offer my prayer to you. . . . In the sanctuary of your Temple in Jerusalem, I will give you what I have promised."

2 Chronicles 32:22-23 (about 430 B.C.). Second Chronicles picks up where 1 Chronicles leaves off and describes events from approximately 970–586 B.C., the beginning of King Solomon's rule to the Babylonian Exile after the fall of Jerusalem. This passage reports many people coming to Jerusalem to bring offerings to God following King Hezekiah's victory over Assyrian Emperor Sennacherib.

2 Corinthians 9:12-14 (about A.D. 56–57). Paul says that giving expresses thankfulness to God and promotes a sense of thankfulness to God in the recipients (Jerusalem Christians who are suffering for lack of food), who benefit from the giving of others. Paul says such giving will cause the hearts of recipients to go out to the donors "because of the surpassing grace of God that he has given" to those who give.

Material Thankfulness

Several decades ago a magazine ad pictured a man poised to invade a delectable-looking plate of food. The caption under the steak, baked potato, and peas reminded us that while we were eating dinner that night, 417 people would starve to death.

At Thanksgiving time each fall many Americans remember how rich they are in comparison to a large percentage of the globe's population. Even the 11.7 percent of United States citizens who live below the poverty level (an average of $18,104 annual income for a family of four according to the 2001 income and poverty statistics from the U.S. Census Bureau, the most recent available) enjoy a level of wealth beyond the imagination of the majority of this planet's occupants.

People respond to that recognition of their wealth with one of two attitudes, both of which are reported in Scripture. Some people say, "My power and the might of my own hand have gotten me this wealth." Others say, "Remember that it is the LORD your God who gives you the power to become rich" (Deuteronomy 8:17-18).

One of these attitudes is Christian thankfulness. The other is secular "self-fullness." Which attitude does your financial giving reflect?

Questions for Reflection

1. In what ways do today's Christians affirm and live out the theme that financial giving expresses thankfulness to God?
2. In what ways do today's Christians sometimes disregard this theme?
3. In what ways do today's church leaders sometimes disregard this theme?
4. How does this financial giving theme apply to you personally?

Theme 4

Financial Giving Acts as God's Steward

A beautiful three-panel stained-glass window in the fellowship hall of a church depicts Jesus with a staff in one hand and a lamb in the other. At the bottom of one stained-glass panel are these words: "Your Works Still Live." Below the inscription is a woman's name.

That window illustrates the primary point of every speaker who urges people to give to an endowment fund. Their money becomes a gift that never stops giving. Their money helps support ministries that assure that Jesus' works still live. Endowment gifts are an eternal memorial to the life values and ideals of donors. Endowment gifts allow God's stewards to extend the benefit of these convictions beyond their lifetime. Yet the same applies when we put a check in the offering plate each Sunday. Where could we possibly find a better investment opportunity?

The word *steward*, *oikonomos*, appears first in the Old Testament reference to a man accountable to Joseph, who rose to a high management position in Pharaoh's government. The word *steward* or *stewards* appears twenty times throughout the New Revised Standard Version Bible. Carrying the implication of trusteeship or servant-manager, the word *steward* often refers to a slave who is responsible for something of value such as money, property, goods, or other slaves. A related word, *trustees*, appears in Galatians 4:2.

In New Testament writings, the Old Testament word *steward* takes on theological and metaphorical meanings in Jesus' parables and Paul's letters to the early churches. Paul says in his letters that God entrusts the steward with transmission of the Gospel message (1 Corinthians 4:1-2). In his letters from prison, Paul says this stewardship is every Christian's responsibility and opportunity (Ephesians 3:1-2). Our basic stewardship is not just money; rather, our stewardship as individuals and churches is for the purpose of extending the good news of Jesus Christ to others in our world and helping those who have already folded that gift into their lives to mature in their relationship with Christ.

1 Corinthians 4:1-2 (about A.D. 55–56). Paul applies the concept of steward to himself and to the church at large with regard to "God's mysteries" (proclamation of the gospel) and says, "Moreover, it is required of stewards that they be found trustworthy." (Paul speaks of this basic stewardship of the gospel message again in Ephesians 3:1-2, saying it was given to him as a gift of God's grace.)

Romans 12:1 (about A.D. 56–57). Paul tells the Christians in Rome to "present your bodies as a living sacrifice, holy and acceptable to God." He goes on to describe this living sacrifice as "your spiritual worship." Paul built his analogy from the Old Testament's Israelite custom of burning sacrifices for God to smell. Now that God has sacrificed his Son as atonement for sin, Paul says Christ wants his disciples to live a life of devotion to God. This echoes the familiar Old Testament prophets' statements that God wants financial giving but wants that giving to symbolize giving the whole heart to God, not just giving money.

Luke 12:42-48 (about A.D. 60). Jesus adds to the story from the first part of this long chapter, which describes the foolish man who built barns and filled them with wealth. Jesus stresses the importance of accomplishing God's will by being a good steward of possessions, and he warns of the dire consequences of failing in that servant role.

Matthew 25:14-30 (about A.D. 60–65) suggests that Christians should handle God's resources as though they are their own, so as to obtain the greatest possible return.

1 Peter 4:10 (about A.D. 64). "Like good stewards of the manifold grace of God, serve one another with whatever gift each of you has received."

Hebrews 13:10-21 (about A.D. 67–70). After a several-chapter analogy that says people connect with the new covenant of Christ's sacrifice for sin "by faith," not by keeping the Old Testament's covenant of the law of Moses, the writer says, "Do not neglect to do good and to share what you have, for such sacrifices are pleasing to God." Then the writer promises that God will equip people with every good thing they need to do God's will, and will work "among us" to bring about that which is pleasing in God's sight.

Christian stewardship uses the life God gave you for God's purposes. Your money is a tangible extension of that life. God does not so much call you to give your money as to give yourself. Yet genuinely giving yourself always involves giving that financial extension of who you are.

The dictionary says that *stewardship* means management. If you call yourself Christian, you are in charge of managing God's financial resources. If you view your resources as "mine," you will find it difficult to give money to God's ministries. If you see your money as God's resources, you can decide much more easily how much to give to God's ministries through God's congregation.

Stewardship is not just an opportunity to enter into God's service but an opportunity for God to enter into you. Thus, the foundational challenge of stewardship education is not getting people to give their money. Rather, the challenge is helping people understand that if they genuinely give themselves to God, their money is not their money. It is God's money. They manage it; they do not own it. So their role as a responsible manager involves deciding how to invest God's money in something that accomplishes God's eternal purposes in God's world, God's people, and themselves.

Questions for Reflection

1. In what ways do today's Christians affirm and live out the theme that financial giving acts as God's steward?
2. In what ways do today's Christians sometimes disregard this theme?
3. In what ways do today's church leaders sometimes disregard this theme?
4. How does this financial giving theme apply to you personally?

Theme 5
Financial Giving Supports God's Long-Range Goals

In an old story about a king with four daughters, the king wanted to learn which one was wise enough to succeed him on the thrown. He told the girls he was going away for several years, and he was entrusting to each of them a special gift that would help them rule while he was gone. It was a mystery gift. Each one was to decide what to do with it. Asking them to hold out their hands, he gave each girl a grain of rice.

The first daughter wrapped a golden thread around the important grain of rice and put it into a crystal box. Each day she took it out and looked at it. The second daughter decided to keep her grain of rice safe by storing it in a wooden box under her bed. The third daughter decided that her grain of rice looked like every other grain of rice and couldn't be worth much, so she blew it off of her hand and never thought any more about it. The fourth girl gave the grain of rice serious thought for a year, until she finally saw what she should do with it.

When the king returned several years later, he asked his four daughters what they had done with their grain of rice. Each girl reported in, describing her reasoning behind how she had handled the gift. The father graciously accepted the first three explanations. The fourth daughter said, "I finally realized the meaning of the grain of rice. It was a seed. So I planted it and grew more seeds. Then I planted those and I harvested the crop. Come and look at the results." Taking the king to a nearby window, she pointed. As far as the eye could see, fields of rice grew, enough to feed their small country. The father, seeing her wisdom, chose her to succeed him in ruling the kingdom.

Old Testament writers remind the Israelites of their eternal covenant with God. New Testament writers remind first-century congregations that they are not in business for themselves. Often using analogies of the Old Testament sacrifices in the Temple, New Testament authors remind Christians that they were bought with a price. They are not their own. Their giving is therefore not directed toward accomplishing their personal goals but toward achieving God's goals. They are to invest this gift of life in ways that have long-term, productive consequences for God's purposes.

Financial Giving Provides God's Tent

Exodus 25:1-9 (about 1290–1250 B.C.). The first "capital campaign" for a worship center appears in the Bible's second book. Exodus describes events from approximately 1290–1250 B.C. during Moses' era. Like all successful contemporary building or capital improvement campaigns, Moses conducts it separately and apart from the "annual operating budget campaign," which the Israelites supported through money collected from each age-twenty-or-above male at census time (see Exodus 30:11-16 below).

To construct the sacred tent in which God will live among the Israelites, God speaks through Moses, asking people to give "whatever offerings anyone wishes to give." These include gold, silver, bronze, and many other elements with which to construct the tent and its worship accessories, including clothing for its high priest. In Exodus 35:4-9, 20-29 Moses repeats the request for offerings to make the "Tent of the LORD's presence" and describes the many ways in which the Israelites respond to that request.

Exodus 36:3-7 (about 1290–1250 B.C.). The Israelites respond generously to Moses' request for offerings to build the "the sacred Tent." They bring more than is needed. So Moses sends a command throughout the camp for no one to contribute anything else. "What had already been brought was more than enough to finish all the work."

Exodus 30:11-16 (about 1290–1250 B.C.). To handle the upkeep of the Tent, all men age twenty and above give an offering of a required amount of money each time Moses takes a census. "This tax will be the payment for their lives, and I will remember to protect them." The first recorded census reports 603,550 such men (Exodus 38:26). (The capital campaign monies are separate from the annual operating budget income, illustrating and affirming the value of that procedure, whose practicality is confirmed in thousands of contemporary congregations that get a negative result from not abiding by the idea.)

Exodus 38:24-31 (about 1290–1250 B.C.) reports some of the generous totals from Moses' "Tent of the LORD's presence" capital campaign: 2,195 pounds of gold and 5,310 pounds of bronze. Additionally, 7,550 pounds of silver are used from the "census of the community" offering commanded in Exodus 30:11-16.

Numbers 7:10 (about 1290–1250 B.C.) states that the leaders of the Israelite tribes also bring offerings to celebrate the dedication of the altar in the sacred Tent.

Financial Giving Provides God's Temple

1 Kings 8:1-5 (about 586–539 B.C.). First Kings, written during the Israelites' Exile in Babylon, continues 2 Samuel's coverage of King David's monarchy, which began around 1010 B.C., and that of his son Solomon, which ended around 931 B.C. This passage reports that King Solomon sacrificed large numbers of sheep and cattle in front of the Covenant Box before he moved it and the tent of the Lord's presence into the Temple the king built.

1 Kings 8:62-64 (about 586–539 B.C.) reports that King Solomon sacrificed 22,000 cattle and 120,000 sheep as fellowship offerings the day he dedicated the Temple, plus grain offerings as he consecrated the courtyard area in front of the Temple.

1 Chronicles 22:14 (about 430 B.C.). First Chronicles retells events from approximately 1010–931 B.C. already recorded in the books of Samuel and Kings but told from a different viewpoint. This passage says King David gave four thousand tons of gold and nearly forty thousand tons of silver to his son Solomon to use in building the Temple.

1 Chronicles 29:3-9 (about 430 B.C.) says King David gave (above what he had already given) from his personal property 115 tons of gold and 265 tons of silver for decorating the Temple walls and making utensils.

1 Chronicles 29:10-22 (about 430 B.C.). King David says, after enormous offerings for the Temple's construction in Jerusalem, that he and the leaders who contributed money actually cannot give God anything, because it is God who gave them the wealth.

2 Chronicles 2:4-6 (about 430 B.C.). Second Chronicles picks up where 1 Chronicles leaves off and describes events from approximately 970 B.C., the beginning of King Solomon's rule, to the Babylonian Exile after the fall of Jerusalem in 586 B.C. This passage reports Solomon telling King Hiram of Tyre that he intends to build a temple in which to present continuous offerings of sacred bread and burnt offerings every morning and evening. Yet Solomon admits that he cannot build God a temple because the vastness of heaven cannot contain God. Anthropomorphic (like a human being) characteristics of God are at this point in history giving way to the idea that God is Spirit and is everywhere simultaneously.

1 Kings 7:51 (about 586–539 B.C.). First Kings, written during the Israelites' Exile in Babylon, continues 2 Samuel's coverage of King David's monarchy, which began around 1010 B.C., and that of his son Solomon, which ended around 931 B.C. When King Solomon finished building the Temple, he placed in its storerooms all of the silver, gold, and other items that his father, King David, had dedicated to God (story repeated in 2 Chronicles 5:1). This passage reports what appears to be the first endowment fund.

2 Kings 12:6-16 (about 586–539 B.C.) describes King Joash's capital improvement campaign to repair the Temple that Solomon built. Joash established a special fund (in a box with a hole in the lid), apart and separate from the annual operating budget of Temple and priestly support. Written much later, about 430 B.C., and from a different perspective, 2 Chronicles 24:4-14 repeats this story but adds to it: Joash orders the priests and the Levites to go and collect from the people in the cities of Judah enough money for the annual Temple repairs. This special offering is similar to a roof repair or furnace replacement campaign in contemporary congregations.

Ezra 2:68-69 (about 450 B.C.) describes events at and following the end of the Israelites' Babylonian Exile, which many scholars date 538 B.C. This passage describes the exiles arriving at the Lord's Temple in Jerusalem. The leaders of the clans give freewill offerings to help rebuild the Temple on its old site. Total offerings are 1,030 pounds of gold, 5,740 pounds of silver, and 100 robes for priests.

See Appendix IV for additional examples of this Temple subtheme, "Financial Giving Provides God's Temple."

Financial Giving Provides God's Priests

Leviticus 2:1-16 (about 1290–1250 B.C.) tells the Israelites how to prepare the bread offering and instructs them to share it with the priests, since the priests had no other means of livelihood.

Leviticus 6:14-18 (about 1290–1250 B.C.) says that from the grain offerings people bring, a token is burned on the Lord's altar and "the priests shall eat the rest of it." This is part of a perpetual support system for the priests.

"For all time to come any of the male descendants of Aaron," the priest, "may eat it as their continuing share of the food offered to the LORD."

Leviticus 7:28-36 (about 1290–1250 B.C.) further explains how people's offerings to God are part of the priestly financial support system.

Numbers 4:16 (about 1290–1250 B.C.) says Eleazar, son of Aaron the priest, "shall be responsible for the whole Tent" and its equipment, and for the grain and other offerings "in the Tent that has been consecrated to the LORD."

1 Chronicles 6:49 (about 430 B.C.). First Chronicles retells events from approximately 1010–931 B.C. already recorded in the books of Samuel and Kings but told here from a different viewpoint. This passage summarizes the priestly responsibilities of Aaron and his descendants for offering sacrifices and incense on the Temple altar and for "all the worship in the Most Holy Place."

2 Chronicles 26:16-18 (about 430 B.C.) reports that King Uzziah of Judah (southern kingdom) becomes arrogant and is punished because he burns incense to God in the Temple himself instead of letting the priests who are descended from Aaron do it. Is this an early example of the highly valued contemporary distinction between the authority of church and state?

Hebrews 5:1-9 (about A.D. 67–70). Using metaphors from several Old Testament books, the writer says every high priest is appointed to represent the people in matters related to God, to offer gifts and sacrifices for sins. God called Jesus to be a high priest in the order of Melchizedek. Thus, Jesus "became the source of eternal salvation for all who obey him."

Hebrews 7:1-2, 15-28 (about A.D. 67–70). The writer weaves an elaborate analogy between the early Old Testament priest Melchizedek, who was given by Abraham one-tenth of the spoils taken in battle as he entered the Promised Land, and Jesus, the new high priest, who sacrificed for people's sins "once for all when he offered himself." People benefit from Jesus' sacrifice by faith in Jesus, "mediator of a new covenant" (Hebrews 9:15).

See Appendix V for additional examples of this subtheme, "Financial Giving Provides for God's Priests."

Financial Giving Provides God's Levites

Numbers 3:1-13 (about 1290–1250 B.C.) during Moses' era shows God's appointment of the Levites (one of the twelve tribes of Israel) to assist the priests in preparing and making the various offerings. "When I killed all the first-born of the Egyptians, I consecrated as my own the oldest son of each Israelite family and the first-born of every animal. Now, instead of having the first-born sons of Israel as my own, I have the Levites; they will belong to me."

Numbers 3:40-51 (about 1290–1250 B.C.) re-explains the appointment of the Levites to assist the priests in preparing and making the various offerings.

Numbers 8:8-19 (about 1290–1250 B.C.) prescribes the offerings and procedures for the Levites' purification and dedication ceremonies as God sets them apart "to work in the Tent for the people of Israel."

Deuteronomy 18:1-2 (about 1290–1250 B.C.) during Moses' era reminds the Israelites that the priestly tribe of Levi is "to live on the offerings and other sacrifices given to the LORD."

Deuteronomy 33:8-10 (about 1290–1250 B.C.) says the Levites are to teach people to obey the Law and "offer sacrifices on your altar."

1 Chronicles 23:25-32 (about 430 B.C.) says that King David sets aside the Levites for all time to care for the various offerings given and burned in the Temple, to weigh and measure the Temple offerings, and to care for the building and everything sacred in it. This seems similar to contemporary churches that appoint trustees or property committees.

1 Chronicles 26:20-28 (about 430 B.C.) says King David delegates to various Levite families the responsibility for the Temple treasury and the storerooms of gifts dedicated to God.

See Appendix VI for additional examples of this subtheme, "Financial Giving Provides for God's Levites."

Financial Giving Provides God's Apostles

Galatians 6:6 (about A.D. 48). The writer reminds these early Christians that they should financially support those among them who teach the Scriptures.

2 Corinthians 11:7-9 (about A.D. 56–57). Paul reminds the Corinthian Christians that "friends who came from Macedonia" paid for his ministry in founding the Corinthian congregation. This remark demonstrates that financial giving to accomplish the church's missionary expansion began early in Christian history.

Luke 8:3 (about A.D. 60) lists several women who provided for Jesus and the twelve "out of their resources."

Philippians 2:17-18 (about A.D. 61). Paul spiritualizes the idea of Old Testament offerings with a metaphor: He says he is joyfully willing to pour out his life's blood on the sacrifice that the Philippians' faith offers to God. Paul urges them to do likewise.

Philippians 4:14-19 (about A.D. 61). Paul repeats his metaphor of a spiritualized burnt offering from Old Testament literature as he thanks the church for their support of his ministry. This was the only church that helped him when he was in Thessalonica: "I have received from Epaphroditus the gifts you sent, a fragrant offering, a sacrifice acceptable and pleasing to God." Paul follows that thankful metaphor with assurance that God will bless the donors for sending it: "And my God will fully satisfy every need of yours according to his riches in glory in Christ Jesus."

1 Timothy 5:17-18 (about A.D. 62–63). Paul affirms the need for Christians to financially support those among them who teach God's Word.

2 Timothy 4:6-8 (about A.D. 66–67). Paul again uses the metaphor of an Old Testament sacrifice. This time he uses a drink offering to describe the end of his life: "I am already being poured out as a libation." He feels he will soon depart for "the crown of righteousness" after having "fought the good fight" and "finished the race."

God's Leaders Help People Put God First

1 Samuel 9:11-25 (about 586–539 B.C.) describes Samuel offering a sacrifice on a worship altar outside a city in the Zuph region as he prepares to tell Saul he will become king of Israel.

1 Samuel 10:3-8 (about 586–539 B.C.) tells of God's Spirit transforming Saul in preparation for Samuel giving "burnt sacrifices and fellowship sacrifices" and secretly anointing him Israel's king at Gilgal.

1 Samuel 11:15 (about 586–539 B.C.) says that the Israelites offer fellowship sacrifices as they proclaim Saul king at Gilgal.

1 Samuel 13:9-14 (about 586–539 B.C.) tells of King Saul inappropriately offering burnt sacrifices to God (a ritual apparently reserved for Samuel, the priest). Samuel tells Saul that because of this he will not endure as Israel's king. Advocates of separation of church and state find in this text biblical support for their view.

1 Samuel 16:1-13 (about 586–539 B.C.) tells how God instructs Samuel to anoint David to replace Saul as Israel's King. This anointing happens in conjunction with the sacrificing of a calf. "Immediately the spirit of the LORD took control of David and was with him from that day on."

Acts 14:8-18 (about A.D. 63–70). The crowds wanted to sacrifice to Paul and Barnabas after Paul healed a lame man in Lystra, but Paul and Barnabas prevented this. Their message steadfastly maintains that converts must put God first instead of putting important and gifted leaders first.

See Appendix VII for additional examples of this subtheme, "God's Leaders Help People Put God First."

A newspaper story reported that an architect had envisioned and accomplished, with the help of twenty thousand people, the construction of twelve miles of sand castles along the California coast—all the way from Redondo Beach to Marina Del Rea. The plethora of sand castles, moats, pyramids, and statues began rising on Sunday morning, was completed by mid-afternoon, and disappeared with the tide in late afternoon. When someone asked the architect why he organized this effort, he replied that it is the only thing you can see in its beginning, middle, and end all in one day.

Christian stewardship achieves the opposite result. Money given to help accomplish God's purposes never quits having an impact. You may see its beginning and a little of its middle, but you never see its end—not in a day, a year, or a century. Do you want to invest your money in something that counts and something that lasts? Where can you go for a better deal than to God?

Questions for Reflection

1. In what ways do today's Christians affirm and live out the theme that financial giving supports God's long-range goals?
2. In what ways do today's Christians sometimes disregard this theme?
3. In what ways do today's church leaders sometimes disregard this theme?
4. How does this financial giving theme apply to you personally?

Theme 6
Financial Giving Motivates Others to Put God First

A pastor asked a successful retired businessman who had just committed himself to giving $100,000 to a great cause in his church, "Are you comfortable with our publicizing this gift, or would you prefer that it remain anonymous?" The old man thought a moment and said, "It might be good to let people know about it. Perhaps it will motivate some of them to consider giving such gifts."

That wise remark stands on the solid rock of biblical evidence. Again and again throughout its pages the Bible illustrates that positive behavior increases the likelihood of positive behavior by other people. This principle repeatedly plays out on the stage of contemporary giving habits. People who give money to God not only accomplish God's goals but also influence spiritual growth in other people who decide to give by following a leadership example.

1 Chronicles 29:3-9 (about 430 B.C.). First Chronicles retells events from approximately 1010–931 already recorded in the books of Samuel and Kings but told from a different viewpoint. This passage says that King David gives from his personal property (above what he has already given) 115 tons of gold and 265 tons of silver for decorating the Temple walls and making utensils—a rather large "advance gift" for a capital fund campaign. Then David asks, "Now who else is willing to give a generous offering to the Lord?" The leaders respond with 190 tons of gold, 380 tons of silver,

675 tons of bronze, and 3,750 tons of iron, plus precious stones for the Temple treasury. "The people had given willingly to the LORD, and they were happy that so much had been given."

2 Chronicles 35:1-19 (about 430 B.C.). Second Chronicles picks up where 1 Chronicles leaves off and describes events from approximately 970 B.C., the beginning of King Solomon's rule, to the Babylonian Exile after the fall of Jerusalem in 586 B.C. This passage describes King Josiah of Judah (southern kingdom) renewing his people's focus on God by reinstituting Temple practices and celebrating the Passover. King Josiah contributes 30,000 sheep and goats and 3,000 bulls. Many other people contribute lambs, goats, and bulls.

2 Corinthians 9:1-2 (about A.D. 56–57). Paul says the generous giving of the disciples in Corinth motivated Macedonian disciples to give.

Someone said that the lives of people in our culture are guided by three questions: So what? Who cares? How can I get mine? Someone else claimed that that is not accurate but that people live by these three questions: Is it easy? Is it fun? What's in it for me?

Neither of those cynics accurately describes the thinking and behavior of vast numbers of Americans. Philanthropic giving has steadily increased for several decades. The incredible response to natural- and criminal-created disasters indicates that far more selfless motives drive much human behavior. The September 11, 2001, disaster in New York City is a fresh indicator of this phenomenon. A survey in January 2002 reported that forty-eight percent of people said they are now more likely to help poverty-stricken Americans than they were before. The generous giving of people to assist those affected by that tragedy inclined many people to give, not just to that cause but to other worthy causes.

Heroes play an important role in human life. Heroes often help people find and live out the best qualities in themselves. Do you want to motivate people to give? Tell stories of people who gave to a great cause. Tell the results that giving accomplished. Tell the results that giving accomplished in the donor's life. People are not basically selfish. They are basically compassionate and generous. When they see compassion and generosity in others, they are more likely to find it in themselves.

Questions for Reflection

1. In what ways do today's Christians affirm and live out the theme that financial giving motivates others to put God first?
2. In what ways do today's Christians sometimes disregard this theme?
3. In what ways do today's church leaders sometimes disregard this theme?
4. How does this financial giving theme apply to you personally?

Theme 7

Financial Giving to God Must Include Helping People in Need

John Wesley's theology of stewardship encouraged Methodists to work with diligence and discipline to make money but live on as little as possible. Wesley set an example with his own life. His inexpensive, simple living was countercultural in his era. Wesley adamantly instructed his followers to give as generously as possible to the poor from the money they saved by frugal living. In this practice, as in so many other ways, Wesley lived out biblical thought and practice.

The Israelite God was remarkably different from the pagan gods worshiped by the tribes among which the Israelites lived. First, Israel's God was "one," demanding that its citizens worship God and God alone. Second, in sharp contrast with the pagan gods, Israel's God demanded righteousness in human behavior. Here in these dim origins of Israelite history appear the first indications of what scholars call *ethical monotheism*. This one God demands righteous behavior (justice and mercy) of worshipers, not just burnt offerings and sacrifices or altars. Jesus and Paul repeat that refrain several centuries later.

Deuteronomy 15:1-11 (about 1290–1250 B.C.) during Moses' era details several ways God commands Israelites to care compassionately for less-fortunate people in their tribes, including lending and in some instances "gifting" money.

Deuteronomy 26:12 (about 1290–1250 B.C.) instructs every Israelite, "Every third year give the tithe—a tenth of your crops—to the Levites, the foreigners, the orphans, and the widows, so that in every community they will have all they need to eat."

Proverbs 11:25 (about 1000–900 B.C.) instructs us to "be generous" and to "help others."

Proverbs 19:17 (about 1000–900 B.C.). "When you give to the poor, it is like lending to the LORD."

Proverbs 21:13 (about 1000–900 B.C.). "If you refuse to listen to the cry of the poor, your own cry for help will not be heard."

Proverbs 22:9 (about 1000–900 B.C.). "Be generous and share your food with the poor. You will be blessed for it."

Proverbs 28:27a (about 1000–900 B.C.). "Give to the poor and you will never be in need."

Isaiah 58:6-8 (about 700–681 B.C.). The Book of Isaiah reports a prophetic ministry before, during, and after the Babylonian Exile (586–538 B.C.), but many scholars date it much earlier. This passage says that God is more pleased with this kind of fasting: "Share your food with the hungry and open your homes to the homeless poor. Give clothes to those who have nothing to wear."

Psalm 112:6-9 (about 499–400 B.C.) says "a good person . . . gives generously to the needy."

James 1:27 (about A.D. 44–46). "Religion that is pure and undefiled before God, the Father, is this: to care for orphans and widows in their distress, and to keep oneself unstained by the world."

James 2:14-19 (about A.D. 44–46). Just before the often-quoted statement that Jesus' disciples are to produce deeds, not just words, James reminds people about a brother or sister who has no clothes or daily food. James says advice to stay warm and feel full has no value unless disciples help with physical needs.

Galatians 2:9-10 (about A.D. 48). Paul says that when the Jerusalem apostles and leaders commissioned Paul and Barnabas for ministry in the Gentile world outside the Jewish synagogues, they stipulated only one requirement, "that we remember the poor, which was actually what I was eager to do."

1 Corinthians 16:1-3 (about A.D. 55–56). Paul reminds the Corinthian Christians about the offering to help needy Christians in the Jerusalem famine. (Repeated in 2 Corinthians 8:1-15 and 2 Corinthians 9:1-5 about 56–57 A.D.)

Mark 10:17-22 (about A.D. 55–65). Jesus tells the young man who scrupulously keeps the Law of Moses but asks Jesus what else he must do to obtain eternal life, "Go, sell what you own, and give the money to the poor, and you will have treasure in heaven; then come, follow me." The young man leaves sad because he has great wealth. (Also recorded in Luke 18:18-23 and in Matthew 19:16-22.)

Mark 12:28-34 (about A.D. 55–65). Jesus says that the most important commandments are to love God with all your heart, soul, mind, and strength and to love your neighbor as yourself. Jesus pronounces the man wise who replies that loving God and neighbor in those ways "is much more important than all whole burnt offerings and sacrifices." (This story is repeated in Matthew 22:34-40 and in Luke 10:25-28, but Luke adds an additional statement from Jesus: "Do this, and you will live.") Can people genuinely love neighbors and be unwilling to give financially to help alleviate their suffering and need?

Luke 3:10-11 (about A.D. 60). Jesus says, "Whoever has two coats must share with anyone who has none; and whoever has food must do likewise."

Luke 19:1-10 (about A.D. 60). Jesus teaches that generosity to the poor is a byproduct of genuinely focusing one's life on God. Zacchaeus says to Jesus, "Look, half of my possessions, Lord, I will give to the poor; and if I have defrauded anyone of anything, I will pay back four times as much."

Luke 10:29-37 (about A.D. 60). Jesus teaches that God-focused people are also neighbor-focused people, focusing even on distant neighbors with unknown names. Jesus' parable tells of a good Samaritan who aids a man who has been beaten and robbed, taking him to an inn and caring for him. Jesus says that before the Samaritan left the inn the next day, he gave the innkeeper two silver coins to care for the wounded man. He promised that whatever more the innkeeper spent to care for the stranger, he would repay when he came back by.

Matthew 25:31-46 (about A.D. 60–65). Jesus equates feeding the hungry, clothing the naked, and caring for the sick with putting God first, thus binding together the two imperatives of his Great Commandment—love God and neighbor.

Acts 6:1-6 (about A.D. 63–70). The Hellenists in the early church complained that "their widows were being neglected in the daily distribution of food." The twelve apostles appointed deacons to handle the distribution, with a laying-on-of-hands ceremony that indicated that the apostles viewed feeding people as a sacred task.

Hebrews 13:10-21 (about A.D. 67–70). After a several-chapter analogy, through which the writer says that people connect with the new covenant of Christ's sacrifice for sin "by faith," not by the Old Testament's covenant of the law of Moses, he reminds them, "Do not neglect to do good and to share what you have, for such sacrifices are pleasing to God." Then the writer adds that God will equip people with everything good for doing God's will, and will work with us to accomplish the things that are pleasing to God.

See Appendix VIII for additional biblical references to this subtheme, "Financial Giving to God Includes Helping People in Need."

In his biography of a famous 1840's British explorer, Edward Rice reports on conditions in Baroda, a city in India. The rulers ranked people below cattle and treated them as such. Girls were considered a liability to the Hindus, so female infants were killed by an overdose of opium or by drowning them in a hole filled with milk. (See *Captain Sir Richard Francis Burton*; Charles Scribner's Sons, 1990; pages 44–45.)

When Christians live up to their biblical mandate, such behavior is not possible. Christians cannot with integrity separate faith from action, loving God and behaving compassionately toward other people. Christians do not have biblically-based faith if their care for the poor and needy is MIA (missing in action). The ethical monotheism of both the Old and New Testaments says that people who love God point caring hands and generous pocketbooks in the same direction as their minds and mouths.

Questions for Reflection

1. In what ways do today's Christians affirm and live out this theme, "Financial giving to God includes helping people in need."
2. In what ways do today's Christians sometimes disregard this theme?
3. In what ways do today's church leaders sometimes disregard this theme?
4. How does this financial giving theme apply to you personally?

Theme 8
Financial Giving to God Must Include Right Living

Supporting your congregation with appropriate financial giving is not the full picture of what God expects of you. Jesus did not tell the rich young ruler only to give his money to the poor. That is only half of this story. Jesus told the young man to give away his money and "come, follow me" (Mark 10:21). Money and the entire self—that is what Jesus asks everyone to give.

Jesus' admonition to the rich young ruler sounds like a radical new idea, but it stands firmly on the centuries-old foundation of ethical monotheism in the Old Testament. Jesus viewed giving money to God without giving self to God in the same way the prophets began to view it hundreds of years earlier. Any attempt to separate money and self is pseudo surgery. Like the prophets who preceded him, Jesus is not satisfied with half a person. He wants all or nothing, not money as a substitute for spiritual commitment to God.

A recurring theme of both Old Testament and New Testament is, People seek and find God; their zeal fades; they fall into pagan worship habits; they then lose their right-living habits; they respond to a prophet, king, or messenger who helps them recover their spiritual focus. The following texts illustrate this recurring theme.

Leviticus 6:1-7 (about 1290–1250 B.C.) reminds Israelites that the sin of cheating or stealing from one another equals sin against God (the recurring

Old Testament theme of ethical monotheism). These verses detail how to repay the wronged person and how to repay God by bringing to the priest "a male sheep or goat without any defects."

Deuteronomy 5 (about 1290–1250 B.C.) gives the Ten Commandments. They summarize the ethical monotheism described up to this point in the biblical drama and preview the developmental stages of Old Testament teaching about offerings. Historically, what the Israelites first give God is burnt offerings, but God wants them to progress to offering righteous living with their entire lives, along with the loving attitude of their hearts.

Psalm 40:6-8 (about 1010–970 B.C.) during King David's era moves beyond the act of giving offerings to assert that God does not want burnt offerings or sacrifices for sin but wants people to do God's will and to follow the instructions in the law that Moses gave the Israelites.

Ecclesiastes 5:1 (about 935 B.C.) in the United Israelite Kingdom (Israel in the north and Judah in the south) sends a sharp, prophetic message little seen in biblical writings until later centuries: "It is better to go there [to the Temple] to learn than to offer sacrifices like foolish people who don't know right from wrong."

Amos 5:21-24 (about 760–750 B.C.). Through Amos, God says right living must accompany right giving. God says he hates the Israelites' festivals, burnt offerings, grain offerings, and the fattened animals they bring him. "Instead, let justice flow like a stream, and righteousness like a river that never goes dry."

Micah 6:6-8 (about 742–687 B.C.). Through the prophet Micah, God says that he finds of little value the calves people burn as offerings to him, the thousands of sheep, and the endless streams of olive oil. Micah says what God "requires of us is this: to do what is just, to show constant love, and to live in humble fellowship with our God."

Hosea 6:6 (about 715 B.C.) reports that God says through Hosea, "I want your constant love, not your animal sacrifices. I would rather have my people know me than burn offerings to me."

1 Samuel 15:3-24 (about 586–539 B.C.) tells of Samuel scolding King Saul because he did not obey God and took the captive cattle to make a sacrifice to God. Samuel says God wants obedience more than he wants sacrifice of the best sheep. "Arrogance is as sinful as idolatry," Samuel tells Saul.

1 Corinthians 13:3 (about A.D. 55–56). Paul warns about giving from a heart that does not put God first and care about neighbor as oneself: "If I give away all my possessions . . . but do not have love, I gain nothing."

Mark 14:3-9 (about A.D. 55–65). A woman anoints Jesus' head with expensive perfume, and some people complain that the perfume could have been sold and the money given to the poor. Jesus says in response that the woman has shown kindness to him while he is still there, just as she and the others can always show kindness to the poor. Thus, Jesus affirms his teaching about the importance of helping the needy from his parable of the sheep and goats (Matthew 25:31-46), and his Great Commandment to love God and love neighbor (Matthew 22:34-40), from a new perspective. These verses are repeated in Matthew 26:6-13 (written about A.D. 60–65) and John 12:1-8 (written about A.D. 85–90). John's Gospel says the woman poured the perfume on Jesus' feet rather than his head, and that it was Judas who complained that the perfume was not sold and the money given to the poor. John adds parenthetically that Judas complained not because he cared about the poor but because he was the keeper of the common purse that paid for the needs of Jesus and the disciples, and he took money from the purse for himself.

Luke 11:42 (about A.D. 60). Jesus says that God condemns people for tithing their income without living righteously. Jesus says they should do both: live righteously and tithe.

Matthew 5:23-24 (about A.D. 60–65). Jesus says that when people offer their gift at the altar in the Temple and someone has something against them, they should leave the gift and go reconcile with that person, then come and offer the gift. Here again, Jesus emphasizes that God expects right behavior toward other people as much as he expects financial gifts. Jesus is echoing the Old Testament's ethical monotheism theme: Worship the one true God and follow his commandments regarding how to live.

See Appendix IX for additional examples of this theme, "Financial Giving to God Includes Right Living."

In the novel *I Heard the Owl Call My Name*, by Margaret Craven, a newly ordained priest has only two years to live. The Bishop sends him to the most difficult assignment he has available, among the Kwakiutl Indians in the seacoast wilds of British Columbia. The young priest patiently succeeds against almost impossible odds, giving of himself steadfastly and slowly gaining the trust of the Indians. The village is never again the same.

At one point in the story, Indian friends take him to a place on the river to which salmon swim to lay their eggs. The salmon have swum out to sea and have returned to the river at the end of their lives to lay their eggs and then die, swimming past new fingerlings that will comprise the next generation. The priest tells a young village woman who finds the scene sad that the whole life of "the swimmer," the Indians' name for the salmon, is one of courage and adventure. When the swimmer dies he has spent himself to accomplish the purpose for which he is made. The priest explains that this is not sadness but triumph.

Success in the Christian life is not defined by whether we live or die but whether we spend ourselves for the purpose for which God designed us. The only potential tragedy is that we die without having lived our life so that something of value sprouts from it. If that tragedy happens, the sadness is not that we die but that we never lived.

Questions for Reflection

1. In what ways do today's Christians affirm and live out the theme "Financial giving to God includes right living"?
2. In what ways do today's Christians sometimes disregard this theme?
3. In what ways do today's church leaders sometimes disregard this theme?
4. How does this financial giving theme apply to you personally?

Part II

How Does Giving Benefit Us?

Theme 9

Financial Giving Reflects Trust in God's Providence

The bottom-line question that Jesus' teachings address is not whether you should be religious or spiritual or become a church-goer. The bottom-line question is: Are you or are you not alone in the universe? Are you or are you not alone in the room where you are reading this page? Is there just you, just what you can see and hear? Or is there something more, something invisible yet knowable, something the generations before you called God?

If you believe Jesus' opinion—that God is here with you, that God loves you as an individual and takes care of you in ways beyond fathoming or predicting—then earmarking a significant segment of your income for God's causes is an easy decision. It never feels like a risky sacrifice of something you may need later.

American money carries the inscription "In God We Trust." If that faith statement is really true for you, financial giving is easy. If it is not true in your mind, financial giving fills you with anxiety rather than joy. When you complete an "estimate of giving" card at your church this year, the bottom line of it is determined by what you have already written at the bottom line of your life. It is either faith or fear, trust or distrust. That, more than your financial means, determines whether you give meagerly or generously.

The Old Testament keeps repeating a theme encountered in its opening book: God takes care of people who worship God, trust in God's providential care, refuse to worship other gods, and live lives of righteous behavior. The following Scriptures illustrate that theme.

Genesis 15:6-11 (about 1290–1250 B.C.). Genesis was written down approximately 1290–1250 B.C. during Moses' era and reports events from an earlier period of history. This passage describes the covenant ceremony between God and Abram that resulted from Abram's trust in the Lord, which was pleasing to God. Abram expresses this trust in his willingness to part with valued animals, with which he and God "cut" this eternal deal. (In Hebrew, the term *make a covenant* actually translates "cut a covenant.") Abram brings a cow, a goat, a ram, a dove, and a pigeon. Except for the birds, Abram cuts each of them in half.

Genesis 15:17-21 (about 1290–1250 B.C.). As the story continues, the Scripture reports that after sunset on the day of the covenant God appears as a smoking fire pot and flaming torch and passes between the pieces of animals. The implication of cutting the animals in two and walking between the pieces is this: If a covenant maker breaks the covenant, the same thing happens to him. Thus the covenant is written in blood. God makes a unilateral promise (requiring nothing from Abram in return): "I promise to give your descendants all this land from the border of Egypt to the Euphrates River."

Exodus 16:22-30 (about 1290–1250 B.C.). During Moses' era the Israelites were reminded to trust God so thoroughly that they set aside one-seventh of their life (every seventh day) to worship him. God promises to reward this "holy day of rest, dedicated to him" with sufficient food to make up for skipping work every seventh day.

Nahum 1:11-15 (prior to 620 B.C.) is a poem celebrating the fall of Israel's oppressive enemy. This passage says, "People of Judah, celebrate your festivals and give God what you solemnly promised him. The wicked will never invade your land again. They have been totally destroyed!"

Luke 12:29-31 (about A.D. 60). Jesus tells his disciples to focus on right living, not financial resources, and says that God will provide for them the material things they need.

Matthew 6:25-34 (about A.D. 60–65). In this chapter, whose earlier verses speak strongly about the why and how of financial giving, Jesus warns people not to allow feelings of anxiety about financial needs to replace (a) faith in God's providential care for their future needs or (b) the aim of right living toward others.

Matthew 17:24-27 (about A.D. 60–65). Jesus tells the disciples that he is willing to pay the required Temple tax, then graphically illustrates that God provides the ability to pay it.

1 Timothy 6:17-19 (about A.D. 62–63). Paul instructs Timothy to tell wealthy people not to trust in their riches but to trust in "God who richly provides us with everything." The wealthy should do good and "be rich in good works, generous, and ready to share, thus storing up for themselves the treasure of a good foundation for the future, so that they may take hold of the life that really is life."

Jesus, like Moses centuries earlier, understood the true source of wealth. It is not creativity, labor, capital, or a stable government, as important as each of those assets is in providing a rich, full life. The true source of wealth is God. When you complete a financial commitment card or give your offering each Sunday, God's providence is what you celebrate—not just your ability to give and the joy that comes from that but also your recognition of God's ability to provide and the sense of security that comes from that.

Questions for Reflection

1. In what ways do today's Christians affirm and live out the theme that financial giving reflects trust in God's providence?
2. In what ways do today's Christians sometimes disregard this theme?
3. In what ways do today's church leaders sometimes disregard this theme?
4. How does this financial giving theme apply to you personally?

Theme 10
Financial Giving Protects Against Materialistic Idolatry

Rudyard Kipling advised the graduating class at McGill University to avoid an obsession with the search for money, power, and fame. Kipling suggested that meeting someone who was not concerned about such things would help them understand how poor they really were.

Kipling's words echo a theme that recurs through the Bible. Giving God the leftover crumbs of your personhood robs you of life's best experiences. Giving yourself and your money wholeheartedly to God's great causes helps counterbalance your natural inclination to worship the god of self.

Both the Old Testament and the New Testament (a) urge us to be industrious and earn money while (b) warning us that selecting money as the central goal of our lives destroys our lives. A purely financial-acquisition approach to life breaks the first commandment, thereby making money a false god that violates our covenant with the true God and increases the likelihood that our pursuit of happiness will end fruitlessly. If you give God only apple cores, what you have left tastes like an apple core.

Proverbs 21:26 (about 1000–900 B.C.) contrasts out-of-focus people ("All they do is think about what they would like to have") with God-focused people ("The righteous, however, can give, and give generously").

Psalm 49:5-20 (about 799–700 B.C.) warns that trusting in wealth to preserve life and create meaning is foolishness, because only God "will save me from the power of death." A familiar contemporary phrase originates in this passage: "His wealth will not go with him to the grave." Giving a portion of income to God protects against the captivity caused by the myth that relationship with money is the primary human need.

Jeremiah 2:11 (about 627 B.C.). The Book of Jeremiah reports a prophet's ministry that began after the northern kingdom of Israel had fallen and while the southern kingdom of Judah (around Jerusalem) was crumbling. This passage says that when people worship false gods, they exchange the real God for gods that cannot help them. Few commentators have better described the results of materialism.

James 5:1-6 (about A.D. 44–46) reminds wealthy people that money can distort values and lifestyles in ways that cause people to miss what is truly important.

Luke 12:14-21 (about A.D. 60). Jesus warns against greed, saying that life does not consist of abundant possessions. He illustrates his point with the story of a rich man who filled his barns and was "not rich toward God" with right living.

Luke 16:9-13 (about A.D. 60). Jesus says people must learn how to use wealth rather than be used up by it. They cannot give equal focus to money and to God. One or the other wins first place in their attention. Whichever gains control of their soul will hold their soul for eternity.

Matthew 6:19-21 (about A.D. 60–65). Jesus warns against an obsession with storing up wealth. Putting God first and right living toward other people are more important than accumulating money.

Philippians 4:10-13 (about A.D. 61). Paul says that in all situations he has learned to be content with what he has.

1 Timothy 6:6-10 (about A.D. 62–63). Paul asserts that the love of money is the root of evil.

1 Timothy 6:17-19 (about A.D. 62–63). Paul instructs Timothy to tell wealthy people not to trust in their riches but to trust in God and give generously "so that they may take hold of the life that really is life."

Sir Winston Churchill (1874–1965) once said, "We make a living by what we get. We make a life by what we give." Churchill had it right. Although your financial giving does not create life, it does protect your life from obsession with trivial irrelevancies that lead to emptiness.

Questions for Reflection

1. In what ways do today's Christians affirm and live out the theme that financial giving protects us against idolizing material wealth?
2. In what ways do today's Christians sometimes disregard this theme?
3. In what ways do today's church leaders sometimes disregard this theme?
4. How does this financial giving theme apply to you personally?

THEME 11

FINANCIAL GIVING BRINGS REWARDS

An apocryphal story tells of two men shipwrecked on an island. Overcome with fear, one said, "We're going to die! We're going to die!" The second man was calm. "Don't worry," he said. "My income is $100,000 a week." The first man was dumbfounded. "What difference does that make? We're on an island with nothing to eat or drink. We're going to die!" "You don't get it!" the second man responded. "I make $100,000 a week. I give ten percent of that to my church. My pastor will find me!"

The biblical record does not support precisely that kind of benefit for people who give generously to God's causes. Yet countless Scriptures say financial giving brings rewards.

Genesis 22:15-18 (about 1290–1250 B.C.) was written during Moses' era. Much of the book describes earlier times during which sacrificing children to pagan gods was a common practice. This first biblical illustration of the reward theme in stewardship makes sense only when readers extract the point the story paints from the dark picture frame that tends to obscure it.

The point of the passage: God rewards people who put God first, trust God, and give without reservation. The text: God promises to profusely bless Abraham and his descendants "because you did this and did not keep back your only son from me" and "because you obeyed my command."

Genesis 28:10-22 (about 1290–1250 B.C.). God promises to bless Jacob, who builds a place of worship and promises to give back to God ten percent of what God gives him.

Exodus 20:22-24 (about 1290–1250 B.C.). The Lord, through Moses, tells the Israelites to sacrifice their sheep and oxen as burnt offerings and offerings of well-being on altars of earth: "In every place that I set aside for you to worship me, I will come to you and bless you."

Deuteronomy 14:22-29 (about 1290–1250 B.C.), after reaffirming the rule that the Israelites give ten percent of their income to God, says "Do this, and the LORD your God will bless you in everything you do."

Proverbs 3:9-10 (about 1000–900 B.C.). This proverb says that if you "honor the LORD by making him an offering from the best of all that your land produces . . . your barns will be filled with grain, and you will have too much wine to store it all."

Proverbs 11:25 (about 1000–900 B.C.). "Be generous, and you will be prosperous. Help others, and you will be helped."

Proverbs 19:17 (about 1000–900 B.C.). "When you give to the poor, it is like lending to the LORD, and the LORD will pay you back."

Proverbs 22:9 (about 1000–900 B.C.). "Be generous and share your food with the poor. You will be blessed for it."

Malachi 3:10 (about 420 B.C.). "Bring the full amount of your tithes to the Temple, so that there will be plenty of food there. Put me to the test and you will see that I will open the windows of heaven and pour out on you in abundance all kinds of good things."

2 Corinthians 9:6-12 (about A.D. 56–57). Paul urges the Corinthian Christians to sow generously, because that produces bountiful reaping. Paul says God rewards generosity by giving the giver all he or she needs: "God is able to provide you with every blessing in abundance, so that by always having enough of everything, you may share abundantly in every good work."

Mark 4:24 (about A.D. 55–65). Whether this statement, "The measure you give will be the measure you get, and still more will be given you," refers to financial giving is not clear. However, that interpretation is consistent with other biblical teachings related to financial giving.

Mark 10:23-31 (about A.D. 55–65). Jesus tells his disciples that it is hard for rich people to enter the kingdom of God, but God can make it possible. Then Jesus predicts that disciples who sacrifice comfort and material wealth will receive more in this present age and receive eternal life in the age to come: Many who are first here will be last there and vice versa. (This discussion is repeated in Luke 18:24-30, and the idea of the first being last and the last being first is repeated in Matthew 20:1-16)

Matthew 6:1-4 (about A.D. 60–65). Jesus says God rewards those who give to needy people.

Matthew 10:42 (about A.D. 60–65). Jesus says God rewards every act of generosity, regardless of how small.

Philippians 4:14-19 (about A.D. 61). In his letter to the church at Philippi, Paul thanks the Philippians for their support of him and his ministry—they are the only church that helped him while he was in Thessalonica: "I have received from Epaphroditus the gifts you sent." He assures them that God will bless the donors for sending it: "And my God will fully satisfy every need of yours according to his riches in glory in Christ Jesus."

1 Timothy 6:17-19 (about A.D. 62–63). Paul tells Timothy to command rich people to be generous and willing to share. By doing so they will lay up treasure for the coming age.

Hebrews 6:10 (about A.D. 67–70) says "God is not unjust" and "will not overlook" efforts to help Christians who do God's will and work.

Contemporary people say that giving brings rewards in three ways. Some givers emphasize the good feeling they get from giving. William Allen White, a famous newspaper editor in Emporia, Kansas, gave the city fifty acres of land for a park. It has been reported that at the park's dedication, the mayor thanked the donor and asked him to say a few words. White remarked that you get three kicks from every dollar. The first kick is when you make it. The second kick is when you save it. The third kick is when you give it away—and this last one is the biggest kick of all.

A second kind of giver stresses the concrete, material compensation for giving. In an old story passed down from the early years of television, a young Catholic boy encouraged his family to respond to an appeal from the well-known television host Bishop Sheen. The family was of moderate means but decided to pool all the money in the house. They came up with $10.35, which was more money at that time than it is today. During the family debate as to whether they should mail it or not, the mother said, "We are going to give it. It will come back to us many-fold." So they sent it. About a week later, the family won a hundred dollars in a local supermarket drawing. At the family council to discuss what they should do with the money, the six-year-old said, "Let's put it all back on Bishop Sheen."

Virtually everyone who gives unselfishly to God's causes affirms that family's experience. Thus the often-heard adage: "You can't out-give God!"

A third kind of giver stresses the eternal value of giving. A funeral procession was passing along a busy street. An armored truck pulled up to the cross-street intersection. Not realizing that the procession of cars was a funeral, the armored car's driver wheeled into the middle of it. A block down the street, a pedestrian said, "What do you know! You can take it with you!"

Biblically speaking, that observer was right. "Store up for yourselves treasures in heaven, where neither moth nor rust consumes and where thieves do not break in and steal," Jesus said (Matthew 6:20).

In which of those three ways do you express the biblical theme that financial giving brings rewards? Do you emphasize the positive personal feeling that comes from generosity? Do you stress the direct material benefit God gives the giver? Do you believe that giving pays off in eternity? All three interpretations stand on the granite foundation of biblical texts.

Unfortunately, unscrupulous religious leaders sometimes abuse this biblical theme. By twisting it to their personal advantage, they give this concept a bad name, encouraging people to support good causes for selfish reasons. Such manipulative maneuvers for selfish purposes by religious con artists discredit their personal integrity. However, promising personal benefit from financial giving is not unscriptural.

Jesus summed up several hundred years of Old Testament teaching and convictions he had expressed on several occasions when he said, "It is more blessed to give than to receive" (Acts 20:35).

See Appendix X for additional examples of the theme "Financial Giving Brings Rewards."

Questions for Reflection

1. In what ways do today's Christians affirm and live out the theme that financial giving brings rewards?
2. In what ways do today's Christians sometimes disregard this theme?
3. In what ways do today's church leaders sometimes disregard this theme?
4. How does this financial giving theme apply to you personally?

Part III

How Should We Give?

Theme 12
Give Intentionally

Sharon said to her husband, "If a doctor ever tells you I have cancer and don't have long to live, I would want you to tell me." "Why?" Ralph asked. "I would want to spend each day the best I could and do all the good I could in the days I had left," the wife replied. Ralph pondered that a few minutes and said, "Why don't you do that anyway?"

The answer is obvious. News of impending death gives people a clear perspective not possible when they think the road ahead is years long. Thus, when nearing death, people often decide to use time and money in ways they should have used them years earlier.

End-of-life conversions to God and good behavior are not a bad idea. However, the Bible suggests that it is a better idea to decide early in life to make good use of time and money. Nowhere in the Bible do readers find encouragement for spur-of-the-moment, emotion-driven giving. The Bible assumes that people who put God first give to God's causes in intentional, planned, carefully thought-out ways. Threaded through both the Old Testament and the New Testament is the injunction to give as one is able, at specific times and in special places.

Deuteronomy 16:16-17 (about 1290–1250 B.C.) says that all the men of the nation are to come and worship and bring a gift to God three times a year—at Passover, Harvest Festival, and the Festival of Shelters.

1 Samuel 20:5-6, 24-29 (about 586–539 B.C.). First Samuel, written during the Israelites' Exile in Babylon, is set in the period between the judges and the monarchy under King David. This passage recalls the annual offering of sacrifices at the New Moon Festival during the years of King Saul and David, who would be his successor.

1 Kings 9:25 (about 586–539 B.C.). First Kings, written during the Israelites' Exile in Babylon, continues 2 Samuel's coverage of King David's monarchy, which began around 1010 B.C., and that of his son Solomon, which ended around 931 B.C. This verse reports that in the Temple he built, King Solomon offered burnt, fellowship, and incense offerings to God on the altar three times each year.

1 Chronicles 16:39-42 (about 430 B.C.). First Chronicles retells events from approximately 1010–931 B.C., already recorded in the books of Samuel and Kings but told from a different viewpoint. This passage describes the place of worship in Gibeon, saying that every morning and evening "they were to burn sacrifices whole on the altar" and mentions the use of trumpets, cymbals, and "other instruments which were played when the songs of praise were sung."

2 Chronicles 8:12-13 (about 430 B.C.). Second Chronicles picks up where 1 Chronicles leaves off and describes events from the beginning of King Solomon's rule to the Babylonian Exile after the fall of Jerusalem, approximately 970–586 B.C. This passage tells of Solomon offering sacrifices on the Temple altar for the various holy days throughout the year.

1 Corinthians 16:1-3 (about A.D. 55–56). Paul reminds the Corinthian Christians to store up their offerings weekly so that when he arrives in Corinth he can send their offerings with messengers to help the needy Christians in Jerusalem.

2 Corinthians 8:10-15 (about A.D. 56–57). Paul urges the Corinthian Christians to give willingly, repeatedly, and according to their means. Paul urges them to give in ways that balance their financial means with the desperate straits of Jerusalem saints who lacked sufficient money to buy food.

Prior to the annual stewardship campaign to support her congregation's ministries through the operating budget, a pastor pointed out the hypocrisy of saying, "I never make pledges; it's against my principles." The pastor supported her conviction by charging that those who say such a thing are liars. "Ask the Iowa Power Company. Ask Southwestern Bell. Ask Visa. Ask the company that holds the mortgage on your house. You say you do not pledge? What you mean is that you do not pledge to God. You do not commit yourself to the support of God's kingdom's ministries."

The Bible does not warn us against making commitments to God's work. Again and again, however, the Bible warns us of the ever-present danger of making strong commitments to small, fake gods, thus leaving God out of our commitment equation.

When you put a dollar amount on your pledge card this year, you are writing much more than how much money you intend to give. You are saying to God, "This is my response to the first of your Ten Commandments: I will have no other gods before you."

Questions for Reflection

1. In what ways do today's Christians affirm and live out the theme that we should give intentionally?
2. In what ways do today's Christians sometimes disregard this theme?
3. In what ways do today's church leaders sometimes disregard this theme?
4. How does this financial giving theme apply to you personally?

THEME 13
GIVE PROPORTIONATELY

Five percent of the United States population has about 25 percent of the country's financial capital. The next 10 percent of the citizens own another 25 percent of the capital. Another 20 percent of the people have another 25 percent of the money, and the remaining 65 percent of people have the remaining 25 percent of financial resources.

This imbalance is not new; it has been around for at least three thousand years. Thus, the Bible keeps repeating the theme "give proportionately." Nothing else makes sense. If God asked everyone to give an equal number of dollars, God would be nuts!

Deuteronomy 16:9-11 (about 1290–1250 B.C.), written during Moses' era, gives specific instructions regarding the celebration of the Harvest Festival: "Honor the LORD your God, by bringing him a freewill offering in proportion to the blessing he has given you."

2 Corinthians 8:10-15 (about A.D. 56–57). Paul urges the Corinthian Christians to give willingly, repeatedly, and according to their means.

Acts 11:27-30 (about A.D. 63–70), part of a history of the early church's expansion, reports the giving of disciples in the Antioch church to help alleviate a coming famine in Jerusalem: "The disciples determined that according to their ability, each would send relief to the believers living in Judea; this they did, sending it to the elders by Barnabas and Saul."

Human needs are enormous. Calls for help seem endless. A man asked his pastor whether there would come a time when he could stop giving. The pastor replied that certainly the man could stop giving—as soon as God stopped giving.

The new member who asked his pastor, "What do most people give?" meant well, but his question was flawed. Likewise, congregations engage in defective solutions when they try to handle a financial crisis by asking every parishioner household to increase its giving by thirty dollars a month to support the next year's church budget. That silly idea (a) is not based on the reality of differing financial resources in each household; (b) always gets poor results; and (c) has no biblical foundation. The Bible teaches proportionate giving, not "divide up the cost of supporting the church and ask everyone to give an equal amount."

Questions for Reflection

1. In what ways do today's Christians affirm and live out the theme that we should give proportionately?
2. In what ways do today's Christians sometimes disregard this theme?
3. In what ways do today's church leaders sometimes disregard this theme?
4. How does this financial giving theme apply to you personally?

Theme 14
Give Regularly

The basic nature of sin is not pride, as some theologians indicate. The essential nature of sin is selfishness. We often tend to express that self-centeredness (sin) by pursuing our own interests first instead of God's interests. When we view our kingdom, not God's kingdom, as having first importance, we have sparse financial resources left over for the causes of God's kingdom.

Mature Christians do not take the love of their possessions and the acquisition of more of them more seriously than the love promised to God at baptism. Mature Christians know that their possessions and their money are temporary and their souls are permanent. Mature Christians have a sense of humor about giving their money to an imperfect institution. Mature Christians know that their financial gift is really to God and not to a less-than-perfect organization with less-than-perfect leadership and management.

Thus, mature Christians follow the biblical injunction to give God their money regularly, not just at the end of the year, the end of the bills, or the end of the time when they are irritated with their current pastor.

The Bible illustrates this theme from its beginning to its ending pages.

Exodus 34:20 (about 1290–1250 B.C.), written during Moses' era, says, "No one is to appear before me without an offering."

Leviticus 23:1-3 (about 1290–1250 B.C.), written during Moses' era, requires the Israelites to forgo earning money on the seventh day of every week and to offer this "Sabbath" to God: "On that day do not work, but gather for worship." When this is coupled with Exodus 34:20 in the above paragraph, God's expectation of weekly financial giving could hardly be more clearly stated.

1 Corinthians 16:1-3 (about A.D. 55–56). Paul reminds the Corinthians to store up their money weekly for the special offering to help the Christians in Jerusalem, who are suffering a food shortage.

Acts 11:29-30 (about A.D. 63–70), part of a history of the early church's expansion, reports the behavior of disciples in the Antioch church in preparation for a famine in Jerusalem: "According to their ability, each would send relief to the believers living in Judea; this they did, sending it to the elders by Barnabas and Saul."

The evidence is clear. The Bible teaches payday giving, not May Day giving ("S.O.S. The ship is sinking; we need money to pay the church's bills"). This regular giving does not mean that churches should never take special offerings to meet a crisis. However, if crisis offerings are a frequent occurrence in your church, most of them are caused by failure to teach the biblical principle of proportionate, regular giving.

Questions for Reflection

1. In what ways do today's Christians affirm and live out the theme that we should give regularly?
2. In what ways do today's Christians sometimes disregard this theme?
3. In what ways do today's church leaders sometimes disregard this theme?
4. How does this financial giving theme apply to you personally?

Theme 15
Give One Tenth

The Bible always defines the tithe as one tenth of one's income. The tithe appears in the earliest Israelite history stories as an appropriate way to put God first, above all other god candidates. Jesus reaffirms giving ten percent in his teachings.

Why, then, do many contemporary Christians disagree about this teaching? The answer to that question is rooted in Christian history, not in the biblical record. In the years after A.D. 312, many of the church's benevolence efforts became part of the Roman government's responsibilities. When the church intertwined with the state—soon termed the Holy Roman Empire—its leaders began to dilute (a) the tithe's purpose and role in helping the poor and (b) the tithe's role in strengthening personal spiritual growth.

A system of tithes was part of a governmental tax system in Europe for centuries, both before and after the Protestant Reformation sprouted wings in 1517, and both in the countries dominated by the Holy Catholic Church and in the countries controlled by Protestant-dominated governments.

Shortly after the Protestant Reformation gathered strength sufficient to dominate the governments of European nations, active resistance to the forced payment of tithes began. A series of events referred to as the tithe wars occurred in England during the 1600's and 1700's. People rebelled against the government officials who collected the tithe and backed their demands with armed force. As late as the 1990's, researchers encountered one Episcopal priest who told them he could not promote the tithe because people in his congregation had bad memories about those wars. (See *Behind the Stained-Glass Windows*, by John and Sylvia Ronsvalle; Baker Books, 1996; page 187).

The idea of a government not married to and supporting the church's clergy salaries and benevolence efforts through taxes is slightly more than two hundred years old. This concept of separating church and state was not part of the Christian landscape between A.D. 312 and A.D. 1776. Thus, church leaders in the United States are plowing new historical ground when they attempt to teach from the biblical record regarding the idea of giving ten percent of one's income to support God's benevolence, mission, and ministry efforts.

To make that effort even more complicated, theological instruction in seminaries since 1776 has relied heavily on the major European theologians such as Aquinas, Luther, and Calvin. Those writers conducted their ministries in state-supported churches. Therefore their focus, consumed by the heated theological issues of their day, was naturally devoid of significant financial stewardship instruction. The European states' marriages to and funding of many of the church's ministries put teaching the Bible's content regarding financial giving low on the list of relevant topics.

What happens if we stop looking through the lens of the church's historical experiences with the concept of tithing? What if we examine what the biblical record says about tithing? We see this subject quite differently.

Genesis 14:17-20 (about 1290–1250 B.C.), written during Moses' era, is the first biblical mention of giving God ten percent of one's material possessions. Abram is victorious over Chedorlaomer and other pagan kings in the land God promised to give Abram and his descendants. Melchizedek, "a priest of the Most High God," conducts a religious ceremony involving bread and wine. Melchizedek blesses Abram and praises God for giving him victory. Then Abram gives "a tenth of all the loot he had recovered" to Melchizedek.

Genesis 28:22 (about 1290–1250 B.C.). After Jacob's dream of a stairway reaching from earth to heaven, he sets up a memorial stone where he will worship God, promising to give God one tenth of everything God gives him.

Leviticus 27:30-33 (about 1290–1250 B.C.), written during Moses' era, states that one tenth of all the Israelites' fruit, grain, and domestic animals belong to the Lord.

Numbers 18:21-31 (about 1290–1250 B.C.), written during Moses' era, says that the Levites, who assist the priests in caring for the tent of God's presence, keep for personal use ten percent of the Israelites' income offerings to God. From that ten percent, God, through Moses, directs the Levites to "present a tenth of it as a special contribution to the LORD." God expects the leaders who ask people to tithe, to tithe themselves.

Deuteronomy 14:22-29 (about 1290–1250 B.C.), written during Moses' era, reiterates the command to "set aside a tithe—a tenth of all that your fields produce each year." The Israelites are to take it to the one place where God has chosen to be worshiped, remembering not to neglect the Levites, who have no property of their own because they serve as God's priestly tribe.

Deuteronomy 26:12 (about 1290–1250 B.C.) instructs every Israelite, every third year, to "give the tithe—a tenth of your crops—to the Levites, the foreigners, the orphans, and the widows, so that in every community they will have all they need to eat."

2 Chronicles 31:2-10 (about 430 B.C.). Second Chronicles picks up where 1 Chronicles leaves off and describes events from approximately 970 B.C., the beginning of King Solomon's rule, to the Babylonian Exile after the fall of Jerusalem in 586 B.C. This passage describes King Hezekiah of Judah (the southern kingdom) reorganizing the priests and Levites to offer burnt offerings and fellowship offerings in the Temple. Along with the many other gifts people give as part of this renewal of Temple worship, the people bring ten percent of everything they have, and large quantities of other gifts. This gives the priests enough to eat, and more than enough of everything they need. (The Law of Moses requires the people to support the priests with offerings.)

Nehemiah 10:32-39 (about 445–432 B.C.). Nehemiah describes the agreement of the people that was made during the time when Nehemiah returned from exile in Babylon to rebuild Jerusalem's walls. This passage describes the people of Israel agreeing to bring various offerings and to give ten percent of their incomes to the Levites and priests, who will place one tenth of it in the Temple storerooms for use in the Temple. The Israelites promise, "We will not neglect the house of our God."

Nehemiah 12:44-47 (about 445–432 B.C.) says that the Israelites give ten percent of their incomes, which is kept in the Temple storehouse to provide support for the priests and the Levites. The people also give "daily gifts for the support of the Temple musicians and the Temple guards."

Nehemiah 13:4-12 (about 445–432 B.C.) tells of a priest, Eliashib, allowing improper use of some Temple storerooms, which renders them ritually unclean. Eliashib apparently has neglected the financial support of the Levites and Temple musicians, who have left town and gone back to their farms. Nehemiah returns to Jerusalem, ritually cleanses the storerooms, and calls the Levites and Temple musicians back to work. The Israelites once again begin bringing ten percent of their grain, wine, and olive oil to the storehouse.

Malachi 3:8 (about 420 B.C.) says it is not right to cheat God "in the matter of tithes and offerings."

Malachi 3:10 (about 420 B.C.). "Bring the full amount of your tithes to the Temple, so that there will be plenty of food there. Put me to the test and you will see that I will open the windows of heaven and pour out on you in abundance all kinds of good things."

Mark 12:41-44 (about A.D. 55–65). Jesus is seated at a place where people put offerings into the Temple treasury. He says that the large amounts the rich people give are not as much in their totality as the penny a poor widow gives, because "she out of her poverty has put in everything she had, all she had to live on." Here again, the Bible asserts that giving is a matter of the heart. God measures generosity by people's willingness to give an appropriate percentage of their financial means, not by the amount they give. (Repeated in Luke 21:1-4.)

Luke 11:42 (about A.D. 60). Jesus says that God condemns people for giving ten percent of their income without living righteously. Jesus says they should do both: live righteously and give ten percent.

Matthew 5:17-20 (about A.D. 60–65). Here Jesus emphasizes that the letter of the Old Testament Law is important, but in the verses that follow (verses 21-48) he goes on to say that the spirit of the heart and right behavior must accompany that letter of the Law. Jesus sees that many of the Pharisees and teachers of the Old Testament Law are not doing these things as they should. Jesus says their actions prevent them from entering the kingdom of heaven (*kingdom of God* and *kingdom of heaven* are synonymous terms). This teaching correlates with Luke 11:42, where Jesus affirms the tithe of one's income but says people must do righteous actions toward one another, not just give ten percent of their incomes.

Matthew 23:23-24 (about A.D. 60–65). Jesus restates an emphasis from earlier in his teaching ministry: People should be committed to "justice and mercy and faith" as well as give ten percent of their spice crop (mint, dill, and cumin). Giving and right living toward God and other people is not an either/or issue.

Pastors and church members sometimes ask, "Why do we find so few New Testament Scriptures affirming the tithe?" That question has a simple answer. Jesus was a Jew. He spent most of his life working in a carpenter shop. Being a Jew, he tithed, just as he honored the Sabbath and adhered to the Old Testament Law. Trying to teach the Jews to tithe would be as relevant as urging them to eat dinner. They already tithed. Jesus saw that the Jews needed to add genuine, heartfelt love of God and neighbor to their religious ritual of tithing. Therefore, Jesus spent most of his instruction time on that topic, accompanied by the assumption that people who genuinely give God their hearts and minds also give God their money.

Questions for Reflection

1. In what ways do today's Christians affirm and live out the theme that we should give one tenth of what we have?
2. In what ways do today's Christians sometimes disregard this theme?
3. In what ways do today's church leaders sometimes disregard this theme?
4. How does this financial giving theme apply to you personally?

Theme 16
Give Generously

After hearing the story of a business tycoon's philanthropic habits, which far exceeded ten percent of his hefty income, someone said, "If I were that rich, I would be generous too!" That quip stands on logic as firm as quicksand. Virtually everyone who gives generously to further God's purposes begins that habit long before they know that wealth is coming in their future. Generosity is rooted in habits of the heart, not in the bank balance.

Urging people to give ten percent is a dangerous legalism that prevents some people from giving generously. The Old Testament describes the tithe as the basic giving level. People also gave offerings above and beyond the tithe. All across the Old Testament's pages, writers urge people to bring their tithes and offerings to God. Teaching this distinction can help wealthy people combat their obvious dilemma: For some people, giving God ten percent of one's income is a covert method of being selfish rather than a means of practicing the Bible's injunction toward generosity.

Exodus 36:3-7 (about 1290–1250 B.C.), written during Moses' era, describes generous giving from the Israelites. Responding to Moses' request for offerings to build the "Tent of the LORD's presence," the Israelites bring more than is needed. So Moses sends a command throughout the camp for no one to contribute anything else. "What had already been brought was more than enough to finish all the work."

Exodus 38:24-25, 29 (about 1290–1250 B.C.) reports some of the generous totals from Moses' "Tent of the LORD's presence" capital campaign: 2,195 pounds of gold, 7,550 pounds of silver, and 5,310 pounds of bronze.

Proverbs 21:26 (about 1000–900 B.C.) defines God's kind of person: "The righteous, however, can give, and give generously."

2 Chronicles 31:2-10 (about 430 B.C.). Second Chronicles picks up where 1 Chronicles leaves off and describes events from approximately 970 B.C., the beginning of King Solomon's rule, to the Babylonian Exile after the fall of Jerusalem in 586 B.C. This passage describes King Hezekiah of Judah (the southern kingdom) reorganizing the priests and Levites to offer burnt offerings and fellowship offerings in the Temple. The people give so generously to this renewal of Temple worship that the gifts pile up. "When King Hezekiah and his officials saw how much had been given, they praised the LORD and praised his people Israel." The high priest, Azariah, says to the king, "Since the people started bringing their gifts to the Temple, there has been enough to eat and a large surplus besides." (These offerings were those required by the Law of Moses: that the Israelites support the priests with offerings since the priests had no other means of support.)

2 Corinthians 8:1-7 (about A.D. 56–57). Paul urges the Corinthian Christians to give generously—as the Macedonian churches did, despite their poverty—because giving is a byproduct of giving oneself to God. Paul weaves together Jesus' two great imperatives—that his disciples love God and love their neighbors—into a call to give unselfishly to others. Paul urges the Corinthians to "excel also in this generous undertaking."

2 Corinthians 8:24–9:5 (about A.D. 56–57). Paul praises the previous generosity of the Corinthian Christians and their eagerness to help. Paul urges them to give "as a voluntary gift and not as an extortion."

2 Corinthians 9:6-12 (about A.D. 56–57). Paul urges the Corinthian Christians to sow generously because that produces generous reaping. He says that people should give what they feel in their hearts, not under a sense of compulsion. They should give cheerfully, because God loves that. God rewards such generosity by giving the giver all he or she needs "so that by always having enough of everything, you may share abundantly in every good work." "You will be enriched in every way for your great generosity, which will produce thanksgiving to God through us."

Romans 12:4-8, 13 (about A.D. 56–57). In his list of gifts that "differ according to the grace given to us," Paul says that those who are gifted as givers should give "in generosity."

1 Timothy 6:17-19 (about A.D. 62–63). Paul instructs Timothy to tell wealthy people not to trust in their riches but to trust in God and be generous, ready to share.

Acts 5:1-11 (about A.D. 63–70), part of a history of the early church's expansion, tells about Ananias and Sapphira conspiring to secretly withhold for private use part of their offering to God. This seems to illustrate that people who put themselves first in place of God do not go unpunished for that self-idolatry.

Acts 8:18-23 (about A.D. 63–70). Peter tells Simon the sorcerer that the gift of the Holy Spirit given to people by God cannot be bought with money. God's power comes to people when they put God first, not when they make contributions without putting God first.

What kind of love would a bride standing at the altar be symbolizing if she gave the groom a wedding ring made of copper? The wise men from the east came to worship the Christ child with generous gifts: gold, frankincense, and myrrh. Olympic competition gives three medals: gold, silver, and bronze. What do we give God? Is it generous, or is it a covert means of selfishness?

Questions for Reflection

1. In what ways do today's Christians affirm and live out the theme that we should give generously?
2. In what ways do today's Christians sometimes disregard this theme?
3. In what ways do today's church leaders sometimes disregard this theme?
4. How does this financial giving theme apply to you personally?

Theme 17
Give Sacrificially

C.S. Lewis said that since there is no easy way to know how much we should give, the safest thing is to give more than we can spare. Building on the Old Testament's foundation, New Testament writings give special emphasis to the virtue of giving sacrificially. Giving sacrificially emulates the behavior of Christ, who gave his life on the cross.

2 Samuel 23:15-17 (about 586–539 B.C.). Second Samuel, written during the Israelites' Exile in Babylon, is a sequel to 1 Samuel, describing the reign of King David and his unification of the northern kingdom (Israel) and the southern kingdom (Judah). This passage tells the story of three brave soldiers. At the risk of their lives, they obtain water for thirsty King David to drink by forcing their way though enemy lines. David pours out the water as an offering to God, saying that to drink it "would be like drinking the blood of these men who risked their lives." (First Chronicles 11:17-19 repeats this story.)

2 Samuel 24:17-25 (about 586–539 B.C.) tells how the prophet Gad instructs King David to deal with his guilty conscience. David buys a threshing place from Araunah and builds an altar to the Lord, on which he gives oxen as burnt offerings and fellowship offerings. Araunah wants to give David the threshing floor, but David insists on paying for it. David says, "I will not offer to the LORD my God sacrifices that have cost me nothing."

1 Kings 17:1-16 (about 586–539 B.C.). First Kings, written during the Israelites' Exile in Babylon, continues 2 Samuel's coverage of King David's monarchy, which began around 1010 B.C., and that of his son Solomon, which ended around 931 B.C. The widow of Zarephath provides food for Elijah the prophet out of her depleted reserves.

1 Chronicles 21:18-30 (about 430 B.C.). First Chronicles retells events from approximately 1010–931 B.C. already recorded in the books of Samuel and Kings but told from a different viewpoint. This passage repeats 2 Samuel 24:18-25, describing how David buys a threshing place from Araunah and builds an altar, on which he gives fellowship offerings and burnt offerings to God. Araunah wants to give David the threshing floor, but David insists on paying for it. David says, "I will not give as an offering to the LORD something that belongs to you, something that costs me nothing." This 1 Chronicles account adds that David is not able to go to Gibeon, the location of the tent of the Lord's presence made by Moses in the wilderness and the altar on which sacrifices were burned. David is "afraid of the sword of the LORD's angel," perhaps because he is still feeling repentant for the guilt that he has admitted earlier in this chapter.

Malachi 1:6-14 (about 420 B.C.). Through the prophet, God reprimands the priests for ignoring the Law of Moses by keeping the best animals for themselves and offering others to God: "When you bring a blind or sick or lame animal to sacrifice to me, do you think there's nothing wrong with that? Try giving an animal like that to the governor! Would he be pleased with you or grant you any favors?"

Malachi 1:13b–2:9 (about 420 B.C.) blames the priests for breaking the covenant by allowing offerings of blemished animals, warning that God will punish their children and will rub the priests' faces in the dung of the animals they sacrifice.

2 Corinthians 8:1-7 (about A.D. 56–57). In his letter Paul urges the Corinthian Christians to give generously. As Paul challenges them to excel in this grace of giving, he uses a theme seen repeatedly in both Testaments: It is God who gives people the power to give.

2 Corinthians 8:8-21 (about A.D. 56–57). Paul encourages generous giving and describes how carefully the person he sends to the Corinthian Christians will administer the gifts they give to help the Jerusalem Christians get through the famine. Paul says he and his assistants "intend to do what is right not only in the Lord's sight but also in the sight of others."

Mark 12:41-44 (about A.D. 55–65). Jesus is seated at a place where people put offerings into the Temple treasury. He says that the large amounts the rich people give are not as much, even when added together, as the penny a poor widow gives, because she "out of her poverty has put in everything she had, all she had to live on." God measures generosity by the percentage people give of their financial means, not by the amount. (Repeated in Luke 21:1-4.)

Ephesians 5:1-2 (about A.D. 60). Paul reminds the Ephesian Christians that "Christ loved us and gave himself up for us, a fragrant offering and sacrifice to God." This metaphor, similar to statements in Paul's letters to other congregations, communicates equally well with Jews steeped in Old Testament Law and pagan Gentiles across the Roman Empire, for whom sacrifices to multiple gods were part of everyday life.

Jesus said the widow's two copper coins exceeded the large gifts of rich people, not in monetary value but in heart commitment. The rich people gave from the top of their pocketbooks, like tipping the waiter at a restaurant. The widow gave from the bottom of her heart, sacrificially, like the poor family scraping by to provide their child a university education. Jesus' point: Whether you loosen your purse-strings or tighten them to support God's ministries depends on what you put first in your life. Does Christ rule, or does King Self rule?

Questions for Reflection

1. In what ways do today's Christians affirm and live out the theme that we should give sacrificially?
2. In what ways do today's Christians sometimes disregard this theme?
3. In what ways do today's church leaders sometimes disregard this theme?
4. How does this financial giving theme apply to you personally?

Theme 18
Give Without Pride

In an English village lived one wealthy family and many poor families. Each winter, the rich family provided an overcoat fund for the poor. The coats were provided free of charge; however, each coat was bright green, the color of the rich family's crest. Genuine Christian giving does not seek recognition for financial contributions. Christian donors recognize their indebtedness to God. They know that their generosity is empowered by God's grace and made possible by God's providential giving of the financial means by which to give.

Some people enjoy contrasting the Old Testament's affirmation of people who take pride in following "legalistic rules" with the New Testament's emphasis on heart-rooted compassionate behavior. Such critics have not sufficiently scrutinized the Bible. The warning against puffed-up pride in financial giving coupled with failure to meet God's expectation of righteous, moral, ethical, and compassionate behavior toward others begins early in the Bible, not late. Jesus did not invent his satirical view of people who take pride in giving right while failing to do right. Jesus vigorously continued a prophetic tradition that was, at a minimum, seven hundred years old.

Amos 4:1-6 (about 760–750 B.C.). The prophetic Book of Amos addresses issues in the northern kingdom of Israel during that period. This passage is a sarcastic treatment of people who carefully practice proper financial giving while disregarding the righteous behavior God expects.

After a list of unrighteous behavior that runs the gamut from oppressing the poor to alcoholism, Amos says: "The Sovereign LORD says, '. . . Go ahead and bring animals to be sacrificed morning after morning, and bring your tithes every third day. . . . Brag about the extra offerings you bring! This is the kind of thing you love to do.'" Amos recounts the message of God that this fake giving and worship has brought famine to their land and that it will bring even worse consequences.

Matthew 6:1-4 (about A.D. 60–65). Jesus says people should give in secret, so that pride and self-righteousness do not become their motives for expressing their love of God through financial giving.

A man who had been honored for his humanitarian work with people with mental retardation did not publicly display his award. He explained that the award was for work he had done yesterday, and he used the award, visible only to him in the privacy of his bedroom, to remind himself daily to ask, "What can I do today?"

Questions for Reflection

1. In what ways do today's Christians affirm and live out the theme that we should give without pride?
2. In what ways do today's Christians sometimes disregard this theme?
3. In what ways do today's church leaders sometimes disregard this theme?
4. How does this financial giving theme apply to you personally?

Theme 19

Give Without Selfish Motives

A British story says a worshiper mistakenly gave a gold pound when he intended to give a shiny, gold-colored penny, which was about the same size. Recognizing his mistake after it was too late, he went to the deacon in charge of the offering, told him about his mistake, and asked to exchange the penny for the pound. The deacon would not believe him. Finally the man gave up and told him to keep the pound, "After all, I gave it to the Lord and He will bless me for it." The deacon replied, "You're wrong about that. God will reward you not for what you gave but for what you wanted to give."

According to the Bible, people who forget themselves in their giving find themselves blessed by God, spiritually and materially, through that forgetfulness. People who seek to serve themselves with their giving lose their wholeness (their spiritual relationship with God) through efforts to attain and preserve personal prestige.

Numbers 22:41–24:25 (about 1290–1250 B.C.) describes the giving of burnt offerings to God in several locations by King Balak of Moab and Balaam, a Mesopotamian diviner hired by King Balak to curse the Israelites as they threaten to invade his territory. After each offering, God protects the Israelites from the potential damage of Balaam's curse by meeting with Balaam and giving him a positive message of wisdom and prophecy regarding the Israelites.

Proverbs 21:27 (about 1000–900 B.C.). "The LORD hates it when wicked people offer him sacrifices, especially if they do it from evil motives."

2 Samuel 15:9-12 (about 586–539 B.C.). Second Samuel, written during the Israelites' Exile in Babylon, is a sequel to 1 Samuel, describing the reign of King David and his unification of the northern kingdom of Israel and the southern kingdom of Judah. This passage tells about Absalom, King David's son, offering sacrifices at Hebron while building a conspiracy to overthrow and replace King David.

1 Kings 1:9-27 (about 586–539 B.C.). First Kings, written during the Israelites' Exile in Babylon, continues 2 Samuel's coverage of King David's monarchy, which began around 1010 B.C., and that of his son Solomon, which ended around 931 B.C. This passage tells of Adonijah conspiring to replace David as king. Adonijah offers a sacrifice of sheep, bulls, and fattened calves and invites other sons of King David and numerous officials to the feast; but he leaves out, among others, Zadok the priest and Solomon, the rightful heir to David's throne.

John 2:13-16 (about A.D. 85–90) tells of Jesus overturning the money-changers' tables and driving the cattle, sheep, and dove salespeople from the Temple with a whip. Jesus' point: Leaders who encourage people to worship and give God money must not try to profit from their financial giving. That behavior puts God last in one's life, not first.

A man who gave one hundred dollars to the building fund at his church was astonished to open his small-town newspaper and find his name on a list of people who gave one thousand dollars. He called the pastor and told him he had given only one hundred dollars. The minister replied, "Oh, we're terribly sorry. We'll print a retraction in tomorrow's newspaper." The man replied that this would be quite embarrassing to him. So the clergyman said, "Well, you turned yourself in. I see nothing else we can do." The man replied, "I suppose I'd better give the other nine hundred dollars," which he did.

That extra nine-hundred-dollar gift helped the church's building fund, but it did not help the giver. Self-serving giving has no foundation in the biblical record.

Questions for Reflection

1. In what ways do today's Christians affirm and live out the theme that we should give without selfish motives?
2. In what ways do today's Christians sometimes disregard this theme?
3. In what ways do today's church leaders sometimes disregard this theme?
4. How does this financial giving theme apply to you personally?

Theme 20
Give Joyfully

The story is told of a famous opera singer who had just given an outstanding matinee performance. When fans gathered to offer congratulations backstage, one of them said, "I see by the program that you have to give another performance tonight." "No," said the singer. "I don't have to give another performance tonight." "But it says right here on the program that you have an eight o'clock performance this evening," the fan said. "I do have a performance tonight," the singer replied, "but I don't have to give it. I get to give it."

The biblical record says that appropriately motivated financial giving to God is like that. The donor sees it not as an obligation, a duty, or a responsibility but as a joyful opportunity. He or she "gets to give it."

Numbers 10:1-2, 10 (about 1290–1250 B.C.), written during Moses' era, directs the Israelites to blow two silver trumpets on joyful occasions at religious festivals "when you present your burnt offerings and your fellowship offerings."

Deuteronomy 16:9-11 (about 1290–1250 B.C.), written during Moses' era, instructs the Israelites regarding the Harvest Festival's freewill offering, telling them, "Be joyful in the LORD's presence."

Psalm 54:6 (about 1010–970 B.C.) says the psalmist will both offer God a sacrifice and give God thanks, "because you are good." This attitude combines joyful giving of a sacrifice with a thankful heart.

2 Samuel 6:13-18 (about 586–539 B.C.). Second Samuel, written during the Israelites' Exile in Babylon, is a sequel to 1 Samuel, describing the reign of King David and his unification of the northern kingdom of Israel and the southern kingdom of Judah. This passage tells about David joyfully offering the sacrifice of a bull and a fattened calf when he moves God's Covenant Box to Jerusalem from Baalah in Judah, accompanying these offerings and the trip to Jerusalem with dancing, shouts of joy, and trumpets. When placing the Covenant Box in the tent set up for it in Jerusalem, David again offers "sacrifices and fellowship offerings to the LORD."

1 Chronicles 15:25–16:4 (about 430 B.C.). First Chronicles retells events from approximately 1010–931 B.C. already recorded in the books of Samuel and Kings but told from a different viewpoint. This passage repeats the 2 Samuel 6:13-18 story above. Again, the Israelites accompany the box with shouts of joy, but this account includes two differences. First, King David here sacrifices seven bulls and seven sheep to make sure God will help the Levites who are carrying the Covenant Box. Second, King David blesses the people and gives them bread, roasted meat, and raisins upon the safe delivery of the Covenant Box.

1 Chronicles 29:10-22 (about 430 B.C.) reports that the Temple construction project has received an offering worth several million dollars. King David says that he and the leaders who contributed it are happy to bring God offerings, because they actually cannot give God anything, for it is God who has given them the wealth.

Nehemiah 12:43 (about 445–432 B.C.). Nehemiah describes Nehemiah's return from exile in Babylon and his rebuilding of Jerusalem's walls after 538 B.C. This passage says that on the day Nehemiah dedicates the Jerusalem city wall, people offer many sacrifices and are full of joy because God has made them happy.

2 Corinthians 9:6-12 (about A.D. 56–57). In his letter Paul urges the Corinthian Christians to give because of what they feel in their hearts, not out of a sense of compulsion. They should give cheerfully, because God loves that.

Acts 20:35 (about A.D. 63–70) is part of a history of the early church's expansion. Paul reports that Jesus said there is more happiness in giving than in receiving.

Paul says that God loves a cheerful giver. Of course, other biblical evidence indicates that God also loves you before you become a cheerful giver. However, God does want you to give, but because you want to help God with what God is trying to get done in the world, not because you have read a rule in a holy book that says you have to do it or because you feel pressured by other people in your church to do it.

At the end of his productive life, former president John Adams, who succeeded George Washington in that office, said his faith in God and the hereafter remained unshaken. Adams reduced his fundamental creed to one sentence: "He who loves the Workman and his Work, and does what he can to preserve and improve it, shall be accepted of Him" (letter to Thomas Jefferson; June 18, 1812).

That sums up the biblical reasons for joy in financial giving. Your money helps God's ministries. It helps your hurting and needy neighbor. It helps you grow spiritually in your relationship with the eternal God.

Questions for Reflection

1. In what ways do today's Christians affirm and live out the theme that we should give joyfully?
2. In what ways do today's Christians sometimes disregard this theme?
3. In what ways do today's church leaders sometimes disregard this theme?
4. How does this financial giving theme apply to you personally?

Appendix I

Financial Giving Puts God First

The Bible reports numerous statements, stories, instructions, and teachings related to this theme's six subthemes.

A. Annual, Monthly, Weekly, Daily, and Special Offerings Put God First

Exodus 23:19, written during Moses' era, says, "Each year bring to the house of the LORD your God the first grain that you harvest."

Exodus 24:5-8 depicts Moses sealing the agreement (covenant) between God and Israel with burned sacrifices and sacrificed cattle. The Israelite part of the agreement is to practice right living toward people and God, plus refusal to worship other gods. God's part of the agreement is to take care of the Israelites.

Exodus 30:10 describes an annual purification ceremony for the altar, accomplished by Aaron's sprinkling the blood of "the animal sacrificed for sin."

Exodus 40:29 describes the first burnt offering and grain offering as the Israelites dedicate the tent of the Lord's Presence.

Leviticus 1, written during Moses' era, gives detailed rules for how the Israelites are to make animal offerings. With all such offerings, the Israelites put God first and give themselves to God.

Leviticus 12:6-8 describes the offering women are to bring after childbirth, when the priest shall "perform the ritual to take away her impurity, and she will be ritually clean."

Leviticus 15:13-15, 29-30 describes offerings to be brought by men who have been cured of a discharge from the penis and by women who have had a flow of blood that was not at the time of their monthly period.

Leviticus 16:1-34 details the sin offering Aaron brings on the annual Day of Atonement (now called Yom Kippur, the most sacred day on the Jewish calendar). Aaron comes before God "behind the curtain into the Most Holy Place." The community of Israel then gives Aaron a sin offering of two male goats and a ram. He divides the two goats by lot and burns one of them on the altar as a sin offering. He sends the other goat "off into the desert to Azazel, in order to take away the sins of the people." The meaning of *Azazel* is not clear. Many scholars think it means a desert demon capable of feeding on an animal laden with the sins of an entire people. From a past misreading of the word *Azazel* comes the contemporary term *scapegoat,* which translates more accurately as "escape goat." The two goats, one burned on the altar and one driven into the wilderness, purify the Most Holy Place (the worship area) and atone for the Israelites' sins, maintaining their status as God's holy nation.

Leviticus 19:5-8 indicates that the Israelites must follow specific rules when they give a fellowship offering. If people eat any of the meat after the second day it is offered, "I will not accept the offering." They are "treating as ordinary what is dedicated to me."

Leviticus 19:20-22 describes the repayment offering that purifies a man from sexual sin.

Leviticus 19:23-25. When the Israelites come into the land of Canaan and plant fruit trees, they are to offer all the fruit of them to God in the fourth year and then may eat of the fruit themselves in the fifth year.

Leviticus 22:17-30 indicates that only perfect animals (those with no defects) are acceptable to God as burnt offerings of various kinds.

Leviticus 27:1-27 details numerous regulations regarding various kinds of offerings—animals, people, money, grain, fruit, and property—the Israelites dedicate to God.

Numbers 5:11-28, written during Moses' era, prescribes the methods by which a priest administers a ritual test to a woman whose husband suspects that she has been unfaithful. The husband offers two pounds of barley flour, which the woman hands to the priest, who then performs a ritual test to determine her guilt or innocence.

Numbers 6:9-21 provides the various behavior rules for Israelites who make special vows to dedicate themselves to God as Nazirites. The offering rules are used if a Nazirite is ever defiled in some way, such as being close to a dead person, as a means of rededication.

Numbers 15:1-29 details regulations concerning when, why, and how to do a wide variety of offerings.

Numbers 19:11-22 gives the Aaronite priests instruction for preparing and administering the ritual of purification for people who become ritually unclean by touching a corpse.

Numbers 28:1–29:40 lists the daily and Sabbath offerings and the various offerings for the special days throughout each year.

1 Samuel 6:3-18. First Samuel was written during the Israelites' Exile in Babylon and describes the period between the judges and the monarchy under King David. This passage describes the gold offerings that the kings of Philistia send "to pay for their sins" when they return the stolen Covenant Box of the Lord to the Israelites at Beth Shemesh. It also tells of the Israelites' response of a burnt offering to God.

2 Kings 3:13-20. Second Kings was written during the Israelites' Exile in Babylon and continues 1 Kings's history of the two Israelite kingdoms—Israel in the north and Judah in the south—from the middle of the ninth century B.C. after the reign of King Solomon to 586 B.C. This passage describes the miracle of producing water that God enabled the prophet Elisha to perform "at the time of the regular morning sacrifice" for the northern kings in the war with Moab.

1 Chronicles 16:39-42. First Chronicles retells events from approximately 1010–931 B.C. already recorded in the books of Samuel and Kings but told from a different viewpoint. This passage describes the place of worship in Gibeon, saying that every morning and evening "they were to burn sacrifices whole on the altar," and mentions the use of trumpets, cymbals, and "other instruments which were played when the songs of praise were sung."

2 Chronicles 29:21-35 relates how King Hezekiah of Judah (the southern kingdom) offers bulls, sheep, lambs, and goats as a sin offering for the people.

Job 1:4-5 reports Job offering sacrifices for his children the morning after each feast, fearing that they might have sinned by unintentionally insulting God.

Job 42:7-9 says that God requires Eliphaz and his two friends to take to Job seven bulls and seven rams to offer as a sacrifice, as a way of apologizing to Job and God for not having spoken the truth about God.

Psalm 66:13-15, written during the divided kingdom era (Judah in the south and Israel in the north), says, "I will bring burnt offerings to your house;/I will offer you what I promised./I will give you what I said I would when I was in trouble."

Psalm 76:11 says, "Give the LORD your God what you promised him;/bring gifts to him, all you nearby nations."

Jonah 1:16 describes the sailors' actions after they throw Jonah into the sea during a storm: "This made the sailors so afraid of the LORD that they offered a sacrifice and promised to serve him."

Jonah 2:9 says that in Jonah's conversation with God inside the great fish, he prays, "I will offer you a sacrifice and do what I have promised."

Ezekiel 44:7. The Book of Ezekiel is the words of a prophet who lived in Babylonian exile before and after the fall of Jerusalem in 586 B.C. This passage, which is part of the prophet's vision, says that God condemns the way the people "have profaned my Temple by letting uncircumcised foreigners, people who do not obey me, enter the Temple when the fat and the blood of sacrifices are being offered to me."

Ezekiel 45:15, continuing the prophet's vision, says, "You are to bring grain offerings, animals to be burned whole, and animals for fellowship offerings, so that your sins will be forgiven."

Ezekiel 45:18-20 describes the sin offerings and procedures for purifying the Temple through the sacrifice of a bull without defect. These offerings on the first and seventh days of the first month are on behalf of people who sin unintentionally or through ignorance. "In this way you will keep the Temple holy."

Ezekiel 45:25 says that the ruling prince is to offer sacrifices during the Festival of Shelters identical to those at the Passover Festival.

Ezekiel 46:12 describes a "voluntary offering"—burned or fellowship—made by the ruling prince. This offering is accomplished in the same manner as on the Sabbath.

Ezekiel 46:13-15 describes the daily offering of flour, olive oil, and a lamb in the Temple.

Daniel 9:21 says that while Daniel is praying during the time for offering the evening sacrifice, Gabriel, whom he has seen in an earlier vision, flies down to him and explains a prophecy he has read.

Ezra 6:19-21 describes events following the end of the Israelites' Babylonian Exile. Ezra describes the returned Israelites, along with people living in the land who have given up pagan ways, celebrating the Passover at the rededicated Temple. They kill animals for sacrifice and eat the sacrifices as part of their worship.

Mark 12:13-17. When the Pharisees and some of Herod's officials try to catch Jesus in a trap so that they can have something to report against him to the Roman government, he says, "Give to the emperor the things that are the emperor's, and to God the things that are God's." (Repeated in Luke 20:20-26 and Matthew 22:15-22.)

Luke 2:22-23. Jesus' parents follow the Law of Moses concerning their child: "Every firstborn male shall be designated as holy to the Lord" (see Exodus 13:2, 12). To do this, Joseph and Mary take Jesus to the Temple and offer the required sacrifice of "a pair of turtle-doves or two young pigeons."

Luke 5:12-14. Jesus strongly warns the man he has healed of leprosy to "Go . . . and show yourself to the priest, and, as Moses commanded, make an offering for your cleansing, for a testimony to them." (Also recorded in Mark 1:43-44 and Matthew 8:3-4.)

Acts 21:26. Paul shows his respect for the Old Testament Law of Moses because this is important to the Jerusalem church leaders. Paul participates in a purification ceremony with his Gentile (non-Jewish) traveling companion and in the offering made for each of them at the end of the purification ritual.

B. Giving the Sabbath Puts God First

Exodus 20:9-10. The Book of Exodus describes Moses extracting the Israelites from Egyptian slavery and starting them on the road to nationhood. This passage reports God telling Moses the Sabbath rule that God expects the Israelites to follow every seven days. The Sabbath ritual combines putting God first, worshiping God, and trusting God for financial security. This stems from the Israelites' journey through the wilderness after the escape from Egyptian slavery, as God keeps them alive with manna and quails. God codifies the put-me-first and trust-me imperative in one of the Ten Commandments he gives Moses at Mount Sinai: "You have six days in which to do your work, but the seventh day is a day of rest dedicated to me. On that day no one is to work—neither you, your children, your slaves, your animals, nor the foreigners who live in your country. . . . I, the LORD, blessed the Sabbath and made it holy."

Exodus 31:12-17 reiterates God's instruction to Moses, reminding the Israelites that their offerings include not just money but their means of making money: time and energy. God tells Moses to tell the Israelites that they are to give God one-seventh of each week: "Keep the Sabbath, my day of rest, because it is a sign between you and me for all time to come, to show that I, the LORD, have made you my own people."

Leviticus 23:1-4 requires the Israelites to forgo the opportunity to earn money every seventh day of the week and offer this Sabbath to God: "On that day do not work, but gather to worship."

Leviticus 23:1-44 details the offering of the seventh day to God as well as the preparation of and manner of offerings for the various religious festivals throughout the year.

Deuteronomy 5:12-15, written during Moses' era, cites as one of the Ten Commandments the rule that Israelites are to dedicate one-seventh of their earning power (one day each week) to God. This rule applies to their children, slaves, animals, and any foreigners who live in their country. In this passage, instead of explaining the Sabbath by referring to God resting on the seventh day after creating the earth in six days, the author tells the Israelites that they are to rest on the Sabbath because God rescued them from slavery in Egypt.

Jeremiah 17:26-27. The Book of Jeremiah describes a prophet's ministry that began after the northern kingdom of Israel had fallen and while the southern kingdom of Judah (around Jerusalem) was crumbling. This passage says that the Israelites must put God first. "They must obey me and observe the Sabbath as a sacred day." Otherwise, God will punish them, even if they bring burnt offerings, sacrifices, grain offerings, incense, and thank offerings to the Temple.

C. Idol Worship Puts God Last

Leviticus 17:3-9, written during Moses' era, warns that offerings must be made to God at the entrance of the tent of worship. People who make offerings to false, pagan gods such as the "goat demons" out in the countryside "shall no longer be considered God's people."

Judges 2:2-6. The Book of Judges describes the period of approximately 1250–1010 B.C., between Joshua's invasion of Canaan and the beginning of the monarchy under King David. This passage reports a prophetic warning from an "angel of the LORD" telling the Israelites that they have done the opposite of what God commanded. They must not make an alliance with pagans and must tear down the pagan altars at Bochim (a Hebrew name meaning "those who cry"); otherwise, they will become trapped by the worship of their pagan gods and fall into polytheism. The Israelites cry, seem to repent, and offer "sacrifices to the LORD."

Judges 2:10-19 reports the Israelites' bad memories in the next generation after Joshua's generation has died. They stop worshiping the God of their ancestors and begin serving the pagan Baals.

Judges 3:7 reports that the Israelites once again stray into polytheism. They worship the idols of Baal and Asherah.

Judges 6:22-35 tells about the Lord's angel appearing to Gideon, who builds an altar to God at Ophrah, then at the Lord's instruction tears down his father's altar to Baal and the symbol of Asherah that was beside it. God tells Gideon to build on the top of the now-empty mound "a well-constructed altar to the LORD your God" and burn an offering to God on it. These actions call the Israelites' attention to the powerlessness of Baal, and they rally around Gideon to rescue Israel from wayward pagan polytheism.

Hosea 5:4-7. Because God's wayward people also worship other gods, God says, "They take their sheep and cattle to offer as sacrifices to the LORD, but it does them no good."

Hosea 8:11-13 condemns idol worship. Hosea quips that "the more altars the people of Israel build for removing sin, the more places they have for sinning!" The prophet says the Israelites disregard God's teaching: "They offer sacrifices to me and eat the meat of sacrifices. But I, the LORD, am not pleased with them, and now I will remember their sin and punish them for it."

Hosea 9:4 says that due to the Israelites' idol worship, God will banish them to foreign lands. There, they will not be able to bring their wine offerings and sacrifices to God.

Hosea 10:1-2 reports that the more prosperous the Israelites become, the more altars they build to false idols. God will punish them for this behavior.

1 Kings 11:7-8. First Kings, written during the Israelites' Exile in Babylon, continues 2 Samuel's coverage of King David's monarchy, which began around 1010 B.C., and that of his son Solomon, which ended around 931 B.C. This passage reports that King Solomon turns away from God by building places of worship where his many foreign wives can burn incense and offer sacrifices to their own gods.

1 Kings 12:25-33 says that King Jeroboam of Israel (the northern kingdom), who was chosen king at Solomon's death, fears that if the people go to Jerusalem to offer sacrifices to the Lord in the Temple there, they will kill him and transfer their allegiance to King Rehoboam of Judah (the southern kingdom). Therefore King Jeroboam builds places of worship on hilltops and puts gold bull calves at Bethel and at Dan. He chooses priests from non-Levite tribe families. King Jeroboam also institutes a new religious festival in his northern kingdom and offers on the altar at Bethel "sacrifices to the gold bull-calves he had made," staffing Bethel with priests who have served at the hilltop worship places he has built.

1 Kings 18:25-39 reports how Elijah the priest confronts the prophets of Baal, rebuilds God's altar that has been torn down, puts wood on it, places the pieces of a bull on the wood, and drenches it all with water. Elijah prays and God sends fire down, consuming it all. The prophets of Baal throw themselves on the ground and exclaim, "The LORD is God; the LORD alone is God!"

2 Kings 5:17-19. Second Kings, written during the Israelites' Exile in Babylon, continues 1 Kings's history of the two Israelite kingdoms—Israel in the north and Judah in the south—from the middle of the ninth century B.C. after the reign of King Solomon to 586 B.C. This passage concludes the story of the prophet Elisha curing Naaman of a skin disease. When Elisha will not accept money, Naaman wants two mule-loads of dirt to take home with him, because he "will not offer sacrifices or burnt offerings to any god except the LORD."

2 Kings 10:18-28 tells how King Jehu of Israel (the northern kingdom) tricks the Samaritan Baal worshipers by pretending to offer a sacrifice to Baal, then has his guards and officers kill all the Baal worshipers and tear down their sacred pillar and temple.

2 Kings 12:1-3 tells that, under King Joash of Judah (the southern kingdom that includes Jerusalem), despite his adherence to doing what pleased the Lord, "people continued to offer sacrifices and burn incense" at the pagan places of worship.

2 Kings 14:3-4 reports that King Amaziah of Judah (the northern kingdom) does as his father Joash did: He does what pleases God but does "not tear down the pagan places of worship, and the people continued to offer sacrifices and burn incense there."

2 Kings 15:1, 4 reports continuation of pagan sacrifices under King Uzziah of Judah (the southern kingdom).

2 Kings 15:34-35 reports the same pagan sacrifice conditions in the reign of King Jotham of Judah (the southern kingdom).

2 Kings 16:10-16 describes how King Ahaz of Judah (the southern kingdom) has the priest Uriah install in Solomon's Temple at Jerusalem an exact copy of Assyrian Emperor Tiglath Pileser's altar in Damascus. Ahaz burns animal sacrifices on it, pours the wine offering and the blood of a fellowship offering on it, and sets aside the original bronze altar "to use for divination."

2 Kings 17:32-41 says that the Assyrians who have settled in Samaria worship God but also worship at and offer sacrifices at the pagan places of worship. God warns them about this but they do not listen.

2 Kings 18:1-6 describes the reign of King Hezekiah of Judah (the southern kingdom), who breaks in pieces the bronze snake to which the people have been burning incense.

Isaiah 57:5-8 says God condemns people who give offerings to smooth stones, offer their children as sacrifices, and have sex as part of their fertility-god worship.

Isaiah 65:3-5 says God cannot stand people who "offer pagan sacrifices at sacred gardens and burn incense on pagan altars."

Isaiah 66:3-4 pronounces God's judgment against people who make sacrifices to and give offerings to false gods.

Ezekiel 20:40. This prophet, who lived in Babylonian exile before and after the fall of Jerusalem, writes of God saying to those who will stop worshiping idols, "I will be pleased with you and will expect you to bring me your sacrifices, your best offerings, and your holy gifts."

Ezra 4:1-2. The Book of Ezra describes events at and following the end of the Israelites' Babylonian Exile, which many scholars date at 538 B.C. In this passage enemies come to offer the returned Israelite exiles help in rebuilding the Jerusalem Temple, saying that they have been offering sacrifices to the same God for a long time. However, those who have returned from exile refuse their help. They know that these people worship the Lord but also worship pagan gods.

1 Corinthians 8:4-6. Paul warns the Corinthian Christians about the danger of idolatry. For the Jewish Christians, eating meat previously offered to idols seems particularly despicable, as the Old Testament continually warned them that God condemns people who try to worship both him and idols. From the Jewish-Christian perspective, the sacrifices people give define who they worship. Appropriate sacrifices connect people spiritually with the one God, proclaimed in and by Jesus Christ. Inappropriate sacrifices connect people with something other than God.

D. Human Sacrifice Puts God Last

Judges 11:30-39 reports Jephthah's backsliding into pagan practices by offering his daughter to God as a thanksgiving sacrifice for victory over the Ammonites.

Jeremiah 7:31 says that God has not asked the people to burn their sons and daughters as sacrifices on an altar they have built in the Hinnom valley.

2 Kings 16:1-4 reports that King Ahaz of Judah (the southern kingdom) has neglected doing what pleases God. He has even sacrificed his own son as a burnt offering to idols. He offers sacrifices and burns incense "at the pagan places of worship, on the hills, and under every shady tree."

2 Kings 21:1-7 reports that King Manasseh of Judah (the southern kingdom) sacrifices his son as a burnt offering and places the symbol of the goddess Asherah in the Jerusalem Temple.

2 Kings 23:5-10 reports that King Josiah tears down or desecrates all the pagan altars where people have been offering sacrifices, including their sons and daughters as burnt offerings.

Psalm 106:37-39 tells of Israelites who "offered their own sons and daughters as sacrifices to the idols of Canaan" and who "made themselves impure by their actions and were unfaithful to God."

E. Putting God Last Reaps Negative Consequences

Leviticus 26:14-46, written during Moses' era, says God will severely punish the Israelites and refuse to accept their sacrifices (offerings) if they break God's commandments. This warning counterpoints the chapter's first section (Leviticus 26:1-13), which promises a cornucopia of benefits if they keep God's commandments and avoid idol worship.

Proverbs 20:25. "Think carefully before you promise an offering to God" implies that failure to take God seriously enough to respect offering vows puts something other than God first, an inattention bordering on polytheism—putting other gods before the Lord.

2 Kings 17:5-20. Second Kings, written during the Israelites' Exile in Babylon, continues 1 Kings's history of the two Israelite kingdoms—Israel in the north and Judah in the south—from the middle of the ninth century B.C. after the reign of King Solomon to 586 B.C. This passage reports that the Assyrian emperor, Hoshea, takes the Israelites at Samaria prisoner and deports them to Assyria. God has sent messengers and prophets to warn people in both the northern and the southern kingdoms against worshiping the goddess Asherah and metal bull calves, sacrificing their sons and daughters as burnt offerings to pagan gods, consulting fortunetellers, and breaking all God's laws. They have not listened and are now taken into exile in Assyria.

2 Kings 22:1-20 describes King Josiah (the southern kingdom) finding the Book of the Law in the Temple and responding positively to its contents. Through a woman prophet, Huldah, Josiah receives the message that God will punish Jerusalem because the people "have offered sacrifices to other gods." However, once Josiah has "listened to what is written in the book" and repented, God promises not to punish Jerusalem until after King Josiah dies.

Jeremiah 34:18-19. Jeremiah describes a prophet's ministry that began after the northern kingdom of Israel had fallen and while the southern kingdom of Judah (around Jerusalem) was crumbling. This passage reports that God says, through Jeremiah, that the officials of Judah and Jerusalem, including the palace officials and priests, "made a covenant with me by walking between the two halves of a bull that they had cut in two. But they broke the covenant and did not keep its terms. So I will do to these people what they did to the bull. I will hand them over to their enemies."

Jeremiah 41:5-7 describes the treacherous murder of eighty men who come to offer grain and incense at the Jerusalem Temple from the northern territory of Israel during the tumultuous days when the invading armies of King Nebuchadnezzar of Babylonia have overrun Jerusalem.

Daniel 8:11-12 is a vision of Daniel that describes an army that attacked "the Prince of the heavenly army, stopped the daily sacrifices offered to him, and ruined the Temple. People sinned there instead of offering the proper daily sacrifices, and true religion was thrown to the ground."

Daniel 8:26, continuing Daniel's vision, says that a voice tells him that his vision will not come true for a long time and he is to "keep it secret for now."

Daniel 9:25-27 says, as Gabriel explains a prophecy to Daniel, that Jerusalem will be rebuilt with strong defenses, but a conquering ruler "will put an end to sacrifices and offerings."

Daniel 11:31. An apparition from God of a person wearing white linen clothes tells Daniel by the Tigris River (Daniel 10:4) that soldiers of the evil king of Syria will "stop the daily sacrifices and set up The Awful Horror." According to Daniel 9:27, this is some kind of idol erected at the highest point in the Temple.

Daniel 12:11 continues the proclamation of the person from God wearing white linen clothes: "From the time the daily sacrifices are stopped, that is, from the time of The Awful Horror, 1,290 days will pass."

Joel 1:13 is in a prophetic book that was likely written sometime during the sixth through the fourth centuries B.C., though some scholars say as early as the ninth century B.C. This passage says that due to the locusts, "There is no grain or wine to offer your God." Subsequent chapters describe this locust scourge as God's call to repentance for the Israelites' waywardness.

Luke 12:42-48. Jesus builds on the story of the foolish man who built and filled barns with wealth (Luke 12:16-21) and warns of dire consequences when people fail in their servant role.

Matthew 25:44-46. Jesus equates feeding the hungry, clothing the naked, and caring for the sick with putting God first, thus binding together the two imperatives of his Great Commandment—love God and neighbor. Jesus warns that such care brings rewards and neglecting such care brings dire consequences.

F. Repenting of Putting God Last Brings Forgiveness

2 Chronicles 15:8-12. Second Chronicles picks up where 1 Chronicles leaves off and describes events from the beginning of King Solomon's rule to the Babylonian Exile after the fall of Jerusalem, approximately 970–586 B.C. This passage shows King Asa of Judah (the southern kingdom around Jerusalem) listening to the words of a prophet, reforming pagan tendencies in the land, and offering sacrifices to God in Jerusalem from loot taken in battle. The people make a covenant in which they agree to worship God with all their heart and soul.

Isaiah 43:22-25. God, speaking through Isaiah, forgives the Israelites' sins, even the failure to bring burnt offerings of sheep or incense or the fat of animals.

Isaiah 66:20 uses an analogy in which God promises to bring the Israelites back from distant countries, "just as Israelites bring grain offerings to the Temple in ritually clean containers."

Ezekiel 20:41. To the Israelites that God will bring back from the countries to which they have been scattered, God says, "I will accept the sacrifices that you burn, and the nations will see that I am holy."

Ezekiel 36:38 prophesies that the ruined cities of the Israelites will be as full of people "as Jerusalem was once full of the sheep which were offered as sacrifices at a festival."

Zechariah 14:21. Zechariah describes the years after the prophet Zechariah and the Israelites returned from exile in Babylonia. This passage is part of a message about Israel that God gives Zechariah, predicting a time when Jerusalem will be a light to the nations. These verses imagine a time in the future when such holiness prevails among the people that "the cooking pots in the Temple will be as sacred as the bowls before the altar. . . . The people who offer sacrifices will use them [the cooking pots] for boiling the meat of the sacrifices." Since these actions would be a clear violation of the Law of Moses, this prediction may be an exaggeration to make a point of how great things will be at that time.

Luke 15:11-32. Jesus' parable of the prodigal son makes crystal clear the attitude of God toward people who repent of their misjudgments about where to put God in their lives' priority list.

Appendix II

Financial Giving Worships God

The Bible reports several additional statements, stories, instructions, and teachings related to this theme.

Genesis 28:22. After the dream in which Jacob sees a stairway reaching from earth to heaven, he sets up a memorial stone where he will worship God, promising to give God one-tenth of everything God gives him.

Genesis 31:51-54. Partly to seal an agreement that settles a family argument, partly as an act of worship, and partly as guarantee that he will keep his promise to God, Jacob kills an animal and sacrifices it on the mountain at the boundary-marker stones between the territories of Laban and Jacob.

Leviticus 9:1-7 describes the day after Moses ordains the Aaronite priests and the offerings that are part of the first worship service before God's tent.

Deuteronomy 26:1-11 instructs the Israelites to take the first part of each crop to the priest at the one place of worship, celebrating God's deliverance of the Israelites from Egyptian slavery.

Joshua 22:10-34 describes an altercation between the tribes of Reuben, Gad, and East Manasseh (who have built an altar to God on the west side of the river at Geliloth) and the other Israelite tribes. The three tribes seem in violation of God's admonition not to build altars at places other than the ones chosen by God. The three tribes defend their action by saying that the altar they have built is not for giving offerings or burning sacrifices; they have built it as a memorial stone to remind future generations that their three tribes also have a right to worship the Lord on the east side of the river with burnt offerings and sacrifices "before his sacred Tent," just as the other tribes do. Because this offering-less altar is actually a memorial stone, "a witness to all of us that the LORD is God," they name the stone "Witness." The fuss is better understood when one is armed with the mental perspective of that time period—namely, that worshiping the Israelite God with offerings in more than one location is not possible. That would be polytheism (worship of more than one God) and the tribes therefore must put a stop to it. However, does this incident also mark the first flowering of a radical new idea? Is this the first time some of the Israelites begin to think they can worship and make offerings to the Lord their God in more than one location simultaneously? Maybe, maybe not; but later in their history the Israelites' thinking shifts to thinking of God as Spirit rather than as anthropomorphic (only capable of behaving like a human being)! When that happens, worshiping God in two locations no longer equals worshiping two or more gods.

Judges 21:2-4 reports that the Israelites "went to Bethel and sat there in the presence of God until evening." The next day they built an altar and "offered fellowship sacrifices and burned some sacrifices whole."

1 Samuel 1:19-28 describes Samuel's birth, his dedication to God's service at Shiloh, and the offerings that accompany worship on that occasion.

1 Chronicles 16:29. First Chronicles retells events from approximately 1010–931 B.C. already recorded in the books of Samuel and Kings but told from a different viewpoint. This passage says, "Praise the LORD's glorious name;/bring an offering and come into his Temple."

1 Chronicles 18:9-11 describes King David dedicating the gold, silver, and bronze Joram has brought him "for use in worship, along with the silver and gold he took from the nations he conquered."

Psalm 50:5, written during King Solomon's reign, defines true worship as happening when God's faithful people make "a covenant with me by offering a sacrifice."

2 Chronicles 35:1-18 describes King Josiah of Judah (the southern kingdom) renewing the peoples' worship of God. Josiah "put the sacred Covenant Box in the Temple" and tells the priests and Levites to do what is necessary to become ritually clean and to prepare the sacrifices. The Passover is celebrated, and King Josiah contributes thirty thousand sheep, lambs, and young goats and three thousand bulls. Many other people contribute lambs, goats, and bulls.

Matthew 2:11. The visitors from the east who have followed a star to Jesus present him with expensive gifts: gold, frankincense, and myrrh.

Appendix III

Financial Giving Worships God

The Bible reports numerous statements, stories, instructions, and teachings related to this theme's two subthemes.

A. Proper Offering Preparation Helps People Worship

Leviticus 2:13, written during Moses era, tells the Israelites to "put salt on every grain offering, because salt represents the covenant between you and God."

Leviticus 3 gives instruction for preparing an animal as a fellowship offering. The Israelites are to give all of the fat on the internal organs to God as an offering. Many times in Leviticus the Israelites are told they must not eat any of the blood or fat with this type of offering or eat meat of any kind with blood in it. "This is a rule to be kept forever by all Israelites wherever they live." They viewed blood as life itself, which only God owns and has control over. The fat surrounding the organs was thought to be at the center of a person's being and was viewed as the best part, which also belonged to God.

Leviticus 4 gives detailed instructions for preparing offerings for unintentional sins—by the high priest, the whole community, a ruler, or an individual.

Leviticus 8:14-29 describes the offerings and their preparation on the day Moses ordains Aaron and his sons as priests.

Leviticus 6:12-13 instructs that the fire on the altar where burnt offerings are placed "must be kept burning and never allowed to go out."

Leviticus 10:1-3. Aaron's sons, Nadab and Abihu, give an offering with incense not on the list of what God says is fitting. Fire burns them "to death there in the presence of the Lord" when they make this unholy offering of their own choosing. Here and throughout the Old Testament Scriptures, God, not self or self-preference, comes first.

Leviticus 21:8, 17, 21-22 provides rules for the priests who handle the food offerings to God.

Leviticus 22:1-7, 10-16 stipulates the ways in which the priests (Aaron and his descendants) are to maintain ritual cleanliness so as to appropriately offer the offerings and to be allowed to eat their portion of them.

Deuteronomy 26:1-11, written during Moses' era, instructs the Israelites to take the first part of each crop to the priest at the one place of worship and thankfully celebrate God's deliverance of them from Egyptian slavery.

2 Chronicles 29:3-8. Second Chronicles picks up where 1 Chronicles leaves off and describes events from the beginning of King Solomon's rule to the Babylonian Exile after the fall of Jerusalem, approximately 970–586 B.C. This passage expands on 2 Kings 18:1-6, adding that King Hezekiah of Judah (the southern kingdom) reopens the Temple gates and has them repaired. The King lectures the Levites on the importance of perpetually burning the sacred lamps, burning incense, and offering burnt offerings.

Nehemiah 13:31. The Book of Nehemiah describes Nehemiah's return from exile in Babylon and the rebuilding of Jerusalem's walls after 538 B.C. This passage summarizes Nehemiah's work in the concluding lines of his written record. After listing all the things he has accomplished—one of which was to arrange for the wood used for burning the offerings to be brought at proper times and another of which was "for the people to bring their offerings of the first grain and the first fruits that ripened"—Nehemiah says, "Remember all this, O God, and give me credit for it."

Ezekiel 45:21-24, part of the prophet's vision, describes procedures for sacrifice by the ruling prince of Israel on the fourteenth day of the first month (the beginning of the Passover Festival), which includes olive oil plus several animal and grain sacrifices.

Haggai 2:10-14, in a collection of brief prophetic messages, is an analogy that ends with "so everything they offer on the altar is defiled." Is Haggai arguing the need to give God proper respect by ritually purifying the altar prior to offering sacrifices on it? Some scholars say yes; others offer different explanations.

B. Proper Offering Equipment Helps People Worship

Exodus 28:36-38 states the symbolic meaning behind the priest's turban. Wearing this turban and ornament assures that God "will accept all the offerings" the Israelites bring, "even if the people commit some error in offering them."

Exodus 29:1-40 describes the ordination ceremony by which Aaron and his sons become priests, along with an "offering to take away the sins of the priests," offerings to support the priests, and various kinds of offerings on the different days of the ceremony.

1 Samuel 14:31-35 records construction of the first altar built by Saul, where the Israelites offer slaughtered cattle as repentance for the forbidden practice of eating meat with blood in it.

1 Kings 7:48. First Kings, written during the Israelites' Exile in Babylon, continues 2 Samuel's coverage of King David's monarchy, which began around 1010 B.C., and that of his son Solomon, which ended around 931 B.C. This passage reports that in the Temple King Solomon builds, he constructs the altar, "the table for the bread offered to God," and other accessories of gold.

2 Chronicles 4:6. Second Chronicles picks up where 1 Chronicles leaves off and describes events from the beginning of King Solomon's rule to the Babylonian Exile after the fall of Jerusalem, approximately 970–586 B.C. This passage describes the ten basins in Solomon's Temple used to rinse the animal parts burned as sacrifices.

2 Chronicles 4:19 describes the Temple's gold furnishings, including its altar and the tables for the bread offering to God.

Ezekiel 40:39-43 describes the prophet's vision of the Jerusalem Temple's tables, where animals will be killed to be burned whole as sacrifices for sin and as repayment offerings, after God brings the Israelites back from exile in Babylon.

Ezekiel 43:18-27 describes, from the vision God gives the prophet, the prescription for dedicating the Jerusalem Temple altar after God brings the Israelites back from exile in Babylon. They are to offer young bulls, male goats, and young rams—all without defects—as sacrifices for sin.

Ezekiel 46:19-24, continuing the prophet's vision, describes the kitchen where the priests are to boil the meat offered as sacrifices in the Temple—which is for "sin" or "repayment offerings"—and bake the offerings of flour "so that nothing holy is carried to the outer courtyard, where it might harm the people."

Appendix IV

Financial Giving Provides God's Temple

The Bible reports numerous additional statements, stories, instructions, and teachings related to this theme.

1 Chronicles 28:12-19 tells of David giving his son Solomon plans for constructing the Temple. David tells Solomon how much gold and silver to use in the various utensils and the gold table where "the loaves of bread offered to God" will be placed and how much gold to use in the altar on which incense is to be burned.

2 Chronicles 7:1-7, retelling the report in 1 Kings 8:62-64, tells of King Solomon sacrificing 22,000 cattle and 120,000 sheep as fellowship offerings the day he dedicates the Temple, plus grain offerings as he consecrates the courtyard area in front of the Temple. This Chronicles report adds that when Solomon finishes praying at the Temple dedication, fire comes down from heaven and burns up the sacrifices, and the light of God's presence fills the Temple. When Solomon offers the burned sacrifices, grain offerings, and the fat from the fellowship offerings, the people have given so much that the altar is too small for it.

2 Chronicles 9:11 says King Solomon uses gifts from the Queen of Sheba to build stairs for the Temple and to make harps and lyres for the Temple musicians.

2 Kings 22:3-9 says King Josiah of Judah (the southern kingdom) resumes the capital improvement campaign for Temple repair by collecting the money from people at the entrance to the Temple and giving it to the repairmen. Second Chronicles 34:9-13 retells this story but adds that money is also collected from people in the northern kingdom of Israel and that the Levites supervise the workmen's repairs.

Ezra 1:4, 7, 11. The Book of Ezra describes events at and following the end of the Israelites' Babylonian Exile, which many scholars date at 538 B.C. This passage tells about King Cyrus of Persia commanding his people to give the Hebrews offerings to present at the Temple of God in Jerusalem when they return from exile to rebuild it. King Cyrus also returns the gold and silver bowls taken from the Jerusalem Temple by the invading army in 586 B.C.

Ezra 3:1-6 describes the returned exiles rebuilding the altar at the Jerusalem Temple and reinstituting the entire set of burnt offerings "according to the instructions written in the Law of Moses."

Ezra 3:7-8 tells of the people giving money to pay the stonemasons and the carpenters to rebuild the Jerusalem Temple and sending food, drink, and olive oil to Tyre and Sidon in exchange for cedar trees from Lebanon.

Ezra 6:1-5. In the royal records at Babylon, Emperor Darius discovers the scroll in which King Cyrus "commanded that the Temple in Jerusalem be rebuilt as a place where sacrifices are made and offerings are burned."

Ezra 6:1, 9-10 is part of the decree Emperor Darius of Babylon sends to the governor of the region west of the Euphrates River, telling him to give the priests in Jerusalem "young bulls, sheep, or lambs to be burned as offerings . . . or wheat, salt, wine, or olive oil," so the priests can burn sacrifices and pray for God's blessing on Darius and his sons.

Ezra 6:16-17 tells of the priests, the Levites, the Israelites, and all the others who have returned from exile dedicating the Temple by giving one hundred bulls, two hundred sheep, four hundred lambs, and twelve goats (one goat for each tribe of Israel) as an offering for sin.

Ezra 7:15-24 quotes a document that Emperor Artaxerxes gave to "the priest Ezra, scholar in the Law of the God of Heaven." The Emperor tells Ezra to take with him to the Temple at Jerusalem a great deal of gold and silver offerings. Ezra is to use this wealth to purchase bulls, rams, lambs, grain, and wine and "offer them on the altar of the Temple in Jerusalem." He may use any leftover gold and silver for whatever he and his people feel is in accordance with God's will.

Ezra 8:24-36 describes Ezra giving to the priests a large quantity of silver and gold and the utensils that Emperor Artaxerxes and his officials gave for transport to Jerusalem. They deliver these things to the priests, the Levites, and leaders of the Israelites in Jerusalem. The returning exiles then burn bulls, rams, lambs, and twelve goats as offerings to God.

Appendix V

Financial Giving Provides God's Priests

The Bible reports numerous additional statements, stories, instructions, and teachings related to this theme.

Leviticus 5 describes offering requirements for specific unintentional and intentional sins. The passage spells out different amounts of offerings for rich and poor people. These various offerings seem to go to support the priest, with God receiving a token part of some of them, such as the flour and grain offerings.

Leviticus 6:19-23 specifies the offering an Aaronite priest brings on the day of his ordination and says, "No part of a grain offering that a priest makes may be eaten; all of it must be burned."

Leviticus 7:7-10 details the parts of sin offerings and repayment offerings that the Aaronite priests may eat and says what "must be shared equally among them." This and countless other Scriptures illustrate the writing style (maddening to contemporary readers) of describing an offering, then coming back again and again to tell how the offering originated and add details to the idea.

Leviticus 10:12-15 provides an additional reminder that from the offerings people bring to God, some parts go to support the priesthood.

Leviticus 14:1-2, 10-32 describe various offerings by people the priests are to declare cured of their skin diseases. The priest is to use part of the offerings as personal food.

Leviticus 24:5-9 describes how to make the bread offering to God then replace it with incense, after which the priests are to eat the bread "because this is a very holy part of the food offered to the Lord for the priests."

Numbers 5:5-10 details how the Israelites are to confess their sin and repay someone they have wronged with an additional twenty percent more than the damage. If that wronged person has died and has no near relative, the guilty person gives this payment to the priest (in addition to the ram that is offered "to perform the ritual of purification for the guilty person"). This rule also applies to every special contribution that the Israelites offer to the Lord. "Each priest shall keep the offerings presented to him."

Numbers 18:8-10, 24 is a review of God's plan to set aside part of the Israelites' offerings to support the Aaronite priests and the Levites.

Numbers 16:40 warns the Israelites that only descendants of Aaron should come to the altar to burn incense to the Lord.

Numbers 18:8-20 lists the many special contributions and offerings from the Israelites that Aaron and his descendants may keep for personal use.

Numbers 31:25-31 describes the distribution of the loot taken by the Israelites in their conquest of the Midianites, including the prisoners. Some of the spoils go to the people; some go to the soldiers; some go to Eleazar, the priest, as a special offering to God; some go to "the Levites who are in charge of the LORD's Tent."

1 Samuel 2:12-17. First Samuel was written during the Israelites' Exile in Babylon and describes the period between the judges and the monarchy under King David. This passage describes Eli's sons, as priests at Shiloh, violating Moses' rules for preparing sacrifices to God and treating people and the offerings they bring with disrespect.

1 Samuel 2:27-36 describes God shifting his blessing away from the priests who inherit the role as Aaron's descendants to "those who honor me." "I will treat with contempt those who despise me." No longer do people automatically inherit God's blessing because of their ancestors. Individualism and the consequences of personal behavior are replacing tribalism.

1 Samuel 3:10-14 seems to revert back from individual responsibility to tribalism as God tells Samuel he will punish Eli's descendants forever. "No sacrifice or offering will be able to remove the consequence of this terrible sin."

1 Kings 13:1-3. First Kings, written during the Israelites' Exile in Babylon, continues 2 Samuel's coverage of King David's monarchy, which began around 1010 B.C., and that of his son Solomon, which ended around 931 B.C. This passage tells of God sending a prophet from Judah (the southern kingdom) to denounce the priests whom King Jeroboam (of the northern kingdom) has installed to offer sacrifices. The prophet predicts that God will slaughter the priests the King has appointed.

2 Chronicles 13:1-12. Second Chronicles picks up where 1 Chronicles leaves off and describes events from the beginning of King Solomon's rule to the Babylonian Exile after the fall of Jerusalem, approximately 970–586 B.C. This passage expands on the 1 Kings 12:25-33 report, charging that any person who wants to be King Jeroboam's priest "can get himself consecrated as a priest of those so-called gods of yours" if he has a bull or seven sheep to offer. By contrast, King Abijah of Judah follows the traditions of the Law of Moses. Abijah's priests are descended from Aaron. They offer incense and animal sacrifices burned whole daily, as well as bread on a ritually clean table, assisted by the Levites. King Abijah of Judah (the God-worshiping southern kingdom), at war with the pagan northern kingdom, tells them they cannot win if they fight against the Lord, because they do not offer what God commands in the right way.

2 Chronicles 23:16-18 tells of Jehoiada, a priest, and King Joash of Judah (the southern kingdom) making religious reforms. Jehoiada puts priests and Levites in charge of the Temple, to burn the sacrifices offered to God and be in charge of the music and celebration.

2 Chronicles 30:15-16 describes King Hezekiah leading the priests and Levites in rededicating themselves, offering the Passover sacrifice and burnt offerings, and sprinkling the blood on the altar.

2 Chronicles 31:2-10 describes King Hezekiah reorganizing the priests and Levites to offer burnt offerings and fellowship offerings each morning and evening. The king gives animals from his own flocks for daily offerings, Sabbath offerings, and the New Moon Festival and other festivals. The Israelites bring gifts of their finest grain, wine, olive oil, honey, and other farm produce.

Ezekiel 44:25-27, part of the prophet's vision, says a priest who touches a corpse that is not a family member and becomes ritually unclean must wait seven days and "go into the inner courtyard of the Temple and offer a sacrifice for his purification."

Ezekiel 44:29-30, continuing the prophet's vision, says, "The grain offerings, the sin offerings, and the repayment offerings will be the priests' food, and they are to receive everything in Israel that is set apart for me." People are to give the priests the first loaf of bread as an offering when they bake and should give them the "best of all the first harvest."

Ezra 10:18-44. The Book of Ezra describes events at and following the end of the Israelites' Babylonian Exile, which many scholars date at 538 B.C. This passage reports a list of priests who have promised to divorce their foreign wives, including the notice that they have "offered a ram as a sacrifice for their sins."

Appendix VI

Financial Giving Provides God's Levites

The Bible reports numerous additional statements, stories, instructions, and teachings related to this theme.

Numbers 4:7 says the Levites will always be sure of proper preparation for the offerings, and, "There shall always be bread on the table."

Numbers 7:2–8 13 tells about the wagon offerings that the clan chiefs of the tribes of Israel bring to God for distribution to the Levites, for use in transporting the sacred tent and its contents.

Deuteronomy 26:12 instructs every Israelite, every third year, to "give the tithe—a tenth of your crops—to the Levites, the foreigners, the orphans, and the widows, so that in every community they will have all they need to eat."

Joshua 13:14. The Book of Joshua describes the first stage of the Israelite invasion of Canaan in approximately 1250 B.C. In this passage the Lord tells Moses that the tribe of Levi is to receive for their own use "a share of the sacrifices burned on the altar to the LORD God of Israel."

Joshua 13:32-33 repeats that reminder, adding that this is the reason "Moses did not assign any land to the tribe of Levi."

Joshua 14:4 discusses the division of the land west of the Jordan River, reminding the Israelites that the Levite tribe does not get a portion of that territory but receives "cities to live in, with fields for their cattle and flocks."

Joshua 18:7 repeats earlier statements about the Levite tribe not getting a share of Israelite land like the other tribes, "because their share is to serve as the LORD's priests."

Joshua 21:1-42 details the assignment of forty-eight cities and the pasture land around them to the various Levite clans in the newly conquered land promised by God to the Israelites. These are the cities God promised to the Levites because they serve as God's priests.

2 Chronicles 11:13-17. Second Chronicles picks up where 1 Chronicles leaves off and describes events from the beginning of King Solomon's rule, approximately 970 B.C., to the Babylonian Exile after the fall of Jerusalem in 586 B.C. This passage repeats but expands on the 1 Kings 12:25-33 description of the theological conflict between Jeroboam (king of the northern kingdom of Israel who fostered pagan worship) and Rehoboam (king of the southern kingdom of Judah who leaned toward "the LORD, the God of Israel"). The people who want to worship the Lord follow the Levite priests to Jerusalem in order to "offer sacrifices to the LORD, the God of their ancestors."

Ezekiel 44:11-14, part of the prophet's vision, says the Levites who have deserted God and worshiped idols must be punished "for the disgusting things they have done." They will therefore do "the menial work" that will need to be done in the restored Temple.

Ezekiel 44:15, continuing the prophet's vision, presents God saying that the Levites descended from Zadok have continued to serve God faithfully and will be the ones to "come into my presence to offer me the fat and the blood of the sacrifices."

Appendix VII

God's Leaders Help People Put God First

The Bible reports several additional statements, stories, instructions, and teachings related to this theme.

1 Samuel 26:19 describes David, the future king of Israel, telling King Saul that if God has turned Saul against David, "an offering to him [God] will make him change his mind."

1 Kings 3:15. First Kings, written during the Israelites' Exile in Babylon, continues 2 Samuel's coverage of King David's monarchy, which began around 1010 B.C., and that of his son Solomon, which ended around 931 B.C. This passage reports that after God speaks to him in a dream, King Solomon goes to Jerusalem and stands before the Lord's Covenant Box to offer "burnt offerings and fellowship offerings to the LORD."

2 Chronicles 29:21-35 reports that during his religious reform and renewal program King Hezekiah of Judah (the southern kingdom) offers bulls, lambs, and goats as a sin offering for the people.

Ezekiel 45:16-17, part of the prophet's vision, says the ruling prince of Israel must provide the animals, grain, and wine for the various kinds of offerings for the whole nation at the New Moon Festivals, the Sabbaths, and the other festivals "to take away the sins of the people of Israel."

Appendix VIII

Financial Giving to God Must Include Helping People in Need

The Bible reports numerous additional statements, stories, instructions, and teachings related to this theme.

Psalm 37:21. "Good people are generous with their gifts."

Proverbs 21:3. "Do what is right and fair; that pleases the LORD more than bringing him sacrifices." Is this an old saying that several Old Testament prophets borrow to strengthen the impact of their criticisms of unethical behaviors? Or is it a quip gleaned from a prophet's sermon? Whichever it is, the statement matches the prophets' hyperbolic styles and warnings to avoid substituting financial giving for appropriate behavior. Either way, it proves that many of Jesus' teachings were not new topics; their roots go a thousand years deep.

Isaiah 1:11-23. The Book of Isaiah reports a prophetic ministry before, during, and after the Babylonian Exile (586–538 B.C.), but some scholars date it much earlier, about 700–681 B.C. This passage says that people's offerings and sacrifices at the Temple are meaningless to God if the people do evil and fail to help the oppressed, the orphans, and the widows.

Isaiah 58:10. "Give food to the hungry and satisfy those who are in need."

Ezekiel 16:49. This prophet, who lived in Babylonian exile after the fall of Jerusalem, says the primary sins of Sodom were pride and not caring for the poor.

Romans 12:4-8, 13. Paul urges the Roman Christians to share with God's people who are in need.

Romans 15:25-28. Paul reports on his plans to take the offering for "the poor among the saints in Jerusalem" to those Jewish Christians.

1 Timothy 5:3. Paul advises Timothy to take care of widows who are really in need.

Acts 4:32-35 tells of believers in the early church sharing their possessions. There is "not a needy person among them." They sell land and houses and bring the money to the apostles, who distribute it according to each person's need.

Acts 10:1-4, 31. Cornelius, a centurion, has a vision in which an angel says, "Your prayers and your alms have ascended as a memorial before God." Cornelius later reports this vision to Peter. Here, as elsewhere, the Bible equates giving to the poor with giving to God.

Acts 11:29-30 reports the response of disciples in the Antioch church to a famine in Jerusalem: "The disciples determined that according to their ability, each would send relief to the believers living in Judea; this they did, sending it to the elders by Barnabas and Saul."

Acts 24:17. In his defense before Felix, Paul says, "I came [to Jerusalem] to bring alms to my nation and to offer sacrifices." Here again, Scripture states that loving neighbors in need and putting God first are of equal importance.

Mark 12:28-34. Jesus says that the most important commandment is to love God with all your heart, soul, mind, and strength and to love your neighbor as yourself. Jesus approves of the reply that loving God and neighbor in those ways "is much more important than all whole burnt offerings and sacrifices." (Repeated in Matthew 22:34-40 and in Luke 10:25-28; but Luke adds an additional statement from Jesus: "Do this and you will live.")

Luke 12:32-34. Jesus says that an important aspect of right living for God is giving to help the poor.

John 13:29 demonstrates that Jesus and the disciples were in the habit of giving to the poor out of the "money bag" they used to buy provisions. Here at Jesus' Last Supper, "some thought Jesus was telling Judas to buy what was needed for the Feast, or to give something to the poor."

Hebrews 13:10-17. "Do not neglect to do good and to share what you have, for such sacrifices are pleasing to God."

Appendix IX

Financial Giving to God Must Include Right Living

The Bible reports numerous additional statements, stories, instructions, and teachings related to this theme.

Leviticus 20:8 says, "Obey my laws, because I am the Lord and I make you holy." God makes the Israelites holy by requiring and accepting their offerings, their ritual behavior, their ethical behavior, their moral behavior, their compassion for one another, and their abstinence from pagan practices such as consulting the spirits of the dead.

Deuteronomy 23:17-18 warns that no money earned by being a temple prostitute "may be brought into the house of the Lord your God in fulfillment of a vow."

Amos 4:1-5 seems to address issues in the northern kingdom of Israel during the divided-kingdom period. This passage is a sarcastic treatment of those who give meticulous attention to detail in worship and financial giving while disregarding the righteous behavior God views as important: "Go ahead and bring animals to be sacrificed morning after morning, and bring your tithes every third day. . . . Offer your bread in thanksgiving to God, and brag about the extra offerings you bring. This is the kind of thing you love to do." Focusing on getting it just right in worship liturgy and financial giving does not compensate for failure to put God's righteous-living commandments first in ones' life.

Psalm 51:16-19 is a prayer for forgiveness that says God wants a humble spirit, not just burnt offerings. Then the psalmist expresses a desire to rebuild Jerusalem's walls so that God will receive both those "proper sacrifices" of the heart and "our burnt offerings" at the altar.

Psalm 61:8 seems to add the peoples' promise of appropriate behavior to the giving of offerings: "I will offer you daily what I have promised."

Hosea 4:10. This prophet, whose ministry predated the fall of Samaria (the capital of the northern kingdom), condemns false and wayward priests and predicts circumstances at the time of their downfall: "You will eat your share of the sacrifices, but still be hungry."

Jeremiah 6:19-20. The book of Jeremiah describes a prophet's ministry that began after the northern kingdom of Israel had fallen and while the southern kingdom of Judah (around Jerusalem) was crumbling. This passage says that God does not care for incense, spices, offerings, or sacrifices from people who "have rejected my teaching and have not obeyed my words." In other words, in God's eyes, financial giving cannot substitute for putting God first with right living.

Jeremiah 7:21-23, noting the ancient Mosaic practice in which people worship by burning part of the sacrifice to God, then eating the rest, says that without righteous living they might as well eat all of the sacrifices they burn to God.

Jeremiah 11:15-17 says that the Israelites cannot prevent disaster just by offering animal sacrifices in the Temple. God wants them to keep the covenant with righteous behavior and is angry with their offering of sacrifices to Baal.

Jeremiah 14:12 quotes God as saying, through Jeremiah, that because the Israelites have turned away from God with their unrighteous behavior, "even if they offer me burnt offerings and grain offerings, I will not be pleased with them."

Malachi 2:13-16 says that God no longer accepts the offerings the priests bring him, because they are unfaithful to their wives. This condemnation may also be a tongue-in-cheek analogy of the priests' unfaithfulness to God's covenant.

Malachi 3:1-5 says God will send a "messenger" who will "purify the priests, so that they will bring to the LORD the right kind of offerings," those that will please God, who asks not for one or the other but for both: righteous behavior and offerings.

Matthew 27:3-10. The chief priests refuse to accept Judas's thirty pieces of silver because it is blood money (money derived from putting God last, not first, by violating God's rule about murder). However, they use the money to buy a burial place for foreigners (non-Jews).

Appendix X

Financial Giving Brings Rewards

The Bible reports numerous additional statements, stories, instructions, and teachings related to this theme.

Numbers 31:48-54, written during Moses' era, tells a story whose foundational assumption is clearly that God benefits people who bring him offerings. Several army officers, after the Israelites' Midianite conquest, come to Moses and voluntarily give numerous gold ornaments "to the LORD as payment for our lives. . . . So Moses and Eleazar took the gold to the Tent, so that the LORD would protect the people of Israel."

Deuteronomy 6:17-25, written during Moses' era, warns the Israelites to obey all the laws God gave them (which includes the financial-giving laws); if they do, God "will always watch over our nation and keep it prosperous."

Deuteronomy 15:1-11 states rules for caring compassionately about, and loaning money to, less-fortunate Israelites. This passage then promises, "Not one of your people will be poor if you obey him and carefully observe everything that I command you today."

Judges 20:26-28, 35. The Book of Judges describes the period between Joshua's invasion of Canaan and the beginning of the monarchy under King David, approximately 1250–1010 B.C. The passage describes the Israelites mourning their numerous wartime casualties at Bethel during their war with the Benjaminites and their offering of burnt sacrifices. ("God's Covenant Box was there at Bethel in those days.") God promises victory the next day. It happens; they defeat the Benjaminites.

1 Samuel 2:18-21. First Samuel was written during the Israelites' Exile in Babylon and describes the period between the judges and the monarchy under King David. This passage reports that at the time of annual sacrifice at Shiloh, the priest tells Elkanah and Hannah that God will bless them with other children because Hannah has dedicated Samuel to God's service.

1 Samuel 7:7-11 tells about Samuel's prayer and burnt offering to God, followed by the Israelites' victory over the Philistines.

2 Chronicles 1:6-12, 15-17. Second Chronicles picks up where 1 Chronicles leaves off and describes events from the beginning of King Solomon's rule, approximately 970 B.C., to the Babylonian Exile after the fall of Jerusalem in 586 B.C. This passage says that to begin his reign Solomon brings the people together to worship and has one thousand animals killed and burned on the bronze altar. Then God appears to Solomon and asks, "What would you like me to give you?" Solomon asks for wisdom. God replies that he will give wisdom but will also give great "wealth, treasure, and fame." Solomon becomes so wealthy that in his time "silver and gold became as common in Jerusalem as stone." Great trade and exports drive the country's strong economy under his kingship.

2 Chronicles 7:11-14. God appears to Solomon at night, after his completion and dedication of the Temple. God says he accepts the Temple as the place where people should offer sacrifices to him. God says if people, when in trouble, come there to pray, repent, and turn away from evil doings, God will hear them, forgive them, and make their land prosperous again.

Psalm 54:6-7, written during King David's era, says the psalmist will offer God a thankful sacrifice "because you are good./You have rescued me from all my troubles."

Psalm 56:12-13, from the same period, says, "I will offer you what I have promised;/I will give you my offering of thanksgiving,/because you have rescued me from death/and kept me from defeat."

Proverbs 28:27. "Give to the poor and you will never be in need."

Matthew 6:1-4. Jesus says God rewards people who give to the needy.

Ordering Information

This book and other resources published by Discipleship Resources may be ordered online at www.discipleshipresources.org; by phone at 1-800-972-0433; by fax at 615-340-7590; or by mail from Customer Services, PO Box 340012, Nashville, TN 37203-0012.